Jan
We have had
some great dreams
Ken Austin

AMERICAN DREAMERS

HOW TWO OREGON FARM KIDS TRANSFORMED AN INDUSTRY, A COMMUNITY, AND A UNIVERSITY

KEN AUSTIN

WITH KERRY TYMCHUK

Oregon State University Alumni Association
Corvallis

Published for the Oregon State University Alumni Association
by Oregon State University Press

The paper in this book meets the guidelines for permanence and durability of the Committee on Production Guidelines for Book Longevity of the Council on Library Resources and the minimum requirements of the American National Standard for Permanence of Paper for Printed Library Materials Z39.48-1984.

Library of Congress Cataloging-in-Publication Data

Austin, Ken, 1931–
    American dreamers : how two Oregon farm kids transformed an industry, a community, and a university / Ken Austin ; with Kerry Tymchuk.
    p.   cm
    ISBN 978-0-87071-774-1 (hardcover : alk. paper)
    1. Austin, Ken, 1931- 2. A-dec (Firm) 3. Dental instruments and apparatus industry—United States. 4. Businesspeople—Oregon—Biography. I. Tymchuk, Kerry. II. Title.
    HD9995.D44A343   2015
    338.7′681761—dc23
    [B]
                                                    2014042309

Book design by Cheryl McLean

© 2015 Ken Austin
All rights reserved.
First published in 2015
Printed in the United States of America

Oregon State University Press
121 The Valley Library
Corvallis, OR 97331-4501
541-737-3166 • fax 541-737-3170
www.osupress.oregonstate.edu

OREGON STATE UNIVERSITY
ALUMNI ASSOCIATION

The OSU Alumni Association's mission is to be an indispensable part of Oregon State University by engaging alumni and friends in the life, promotion, and advancement of the university. Our vision is to enrich the lives of alumni and friends by helping them establish lifelong, meaningful, and valued relationships with OSU and with each other.

OSU Alumni Association
204 CH2M HILL Alumni Center
Corvallis, Oregon 97331
www.osualum.com

To Joan: For always. For keeps.

CONTENTS

FOREWORD

Soon after I assumed the presidency of Oregon State University in 2003, I was invited by Ken and Joan (pronounced Jo-Anne) Austin to tour the Newberg headquarters of A-dec, the dental equipment company they founded nearly forty years earlier. I had briefly met Ken and Joan at fall home OSU football games, where my wife, Beth, kept Ken supplied with homemade chocolate brownies. I knew they were wonderfully successful alumni of the university and leading business and philanthropic members of the OSU and Oregon communities. What I did not know, however, was what I learned for the first time on my tour—just how truly unique Ken and Joan were as employers and as individuals, and what an extraordinary team they were. Ken is incredibly creative, has invented many useful devices, and tinkers with a world-class automobile collection. Joan was one of the warmest people I ever met and possessed a very sharp business sense.

We must have crossed paths with three or four hundred A-dec employees as we walked through offices and the manufacturing floor, and Ken and Joan personally greeted each of them by name, treating them like members of their family. I could also see the affection and admiration the employees had for the Austins, and the pride they took in their jobs was palpable. I told Ken and Joan that they were members of the OSU family, too, and whether or not they gave another dime to OSU, I wanted to get to know them better. Over the course of the past decade, it has been my privilege to do just that.

Our time together has included countless meetings and conversations about the future of Oregon State University and how we could better serve our students, and it has included sharing the highs and lows that come with rooting for the Beaver athletic teams. They also spoke to me often about their passion for their community of Newberg and their commitment to support education, job opportunities, and other philanthropic interests. The bottom line is that it was just plain fun to hang out with Ken and Joan. After all, no one could be the first "Benny Beaver," as Ken was, without having a fun-loving side and caring deeply about other people. Ken has those qualities, but it took Joan to help him share that part of himself with others.

Through it all, I came to know Ken and Joan as two of the most visionary and impactful individuals in the nearly a century-and-a-half history of OSU, and as exceptional contributors who have truly improved the lives of generations of students. Indeed, it is impossible to walk more than a few steps on OSU's beautiful campus without seeing ample evidence of the Austins' generosity and leadership.

Perhaps the most impressive piece of evidence is Weatherford Residential College, which is home to the innovative Austin Entrepreneur Program and to some 290 students interested in leadership, professional development, innovation, and entrepreneurship. It is those students, and the many thousands of others who have benefitted from programs and scholarships sponsored by Ken and Joan, who stand as part of their enduring legacy. Their impact on the City of Newberg and the surrounding community is equally wonderful and durable.

I am delighted that Ken is now sharing his and Joan's life story. At its heart, it is a story of the American dream, and how that dream can become a reality through hard work, perseverance, intelligence, and integrity. It is the story of two wonderfully matched personalities and talents. It is a story of genius, love, and service. As you will read, Ken Austin gives a great deal of credit to Oregon State University for his success. The truth is that Oregon State University owes a great deal of credit for our success to Ken and Joan. I can say without hesitation that for as long as there is an Oregon State University, Ken and Joan Austin will be remembered and celebrated with genuine affection.

Dr. Ed Ray
President, Oregon State University

I knew Joan was the one for me when she showed interest in hot-rodding and accompanied me to races as my "pit boss."

PROLOGUE

Though it was over sixty years ago, I still remember every detail. It was June 2, 1952, and I finally had a date with the girl of my dreams. Her name was Joan Zemke, and I first saw her at Newberg High School, where she was a member of the class one year ahead of mine. She was beautiful, popular, intelligent, and usually dating a guy who drove a car newer and better than mine. I was just a poor farm boy, and the truth is I never had the nerve to ask her out because I was certain she would turn me down.

After graduating from high school, I enrolled at Oregon State College in Corvallis. Joan was working for an insurance agency in Newberg, where we would occasionally cross paths when I was home from college. I remained in awe of her, and I also remained convinced that a girl like her would never go out with a guy like me.

Fate intervened the summer between my junior and senior years at OSC. I was returning to Newberg from Eugene, Oregon, where I had competed in a Sunday drag race with my 1927 Model T Coupe. The girl I had been dating—and to whom I had recently given my fraternity pin—was at the race, as was Don Fair, one of my best friends, and his girlfriend, Lenora Zemke, who was Joan's sister. My date found the drag race to be loud and boring, and she immediately presented me with a choice: I could either give up racing or she would give up on me, and I could have my fraternity pin back. I chose the pin. Following the race, Don asked if he could borrow my car to take Lenora out on another date. Newly single and sensing an opportunity, I told Don that the car was his if he could get me a date with Joan. He phoned a few hours later to say that a date had been arranged for the very next night.

Dressed in my finest clothes, I drove to Joan's house that evening, expecting that she, too, would be looking her best. I guessed wrong. Joan had her hair in curlers, was wearing baggy pants, flip-flops, and an old Hawaiian shirt with the sleeves rolled up. Seeing the stunned look on my face, she said, "If you want a real date you need to ask me and not my sister's boyfriend!"

It didn't take me long to learn my lesson. The next afternoon, I asked her if I could pick her up after work in my T Coupe, and she said yes. This time, I had a little surprise for her. The T had no floorboards and was still under construction. Anyone riding in the passenger seat could look down and see the pavement directly beneath them. This fact caused other dates who had stepped into the car to immediately step out in fear. Joan was different. She jumped in and said, "Neat car! What do I do with my skirt?"

If I wasn't in love with her at that very moment, the next several months eliminated all doubt. I had never been with anyone who was so intelligent, understanding, and tender. Unlike my prior girlfriends, she even wanted to be with me when I was working on cars. She would hand me wrenches and stoke the wood-burning stove in the workshop when it was cold. Moreover, without my knowing, she actually began reading books on car repair and would eventually accompany me to several races, where she served as my "pit boss."

The first time I told Joan that I loved her was that September, on the night before I left to race a car at the Bonneville Salt Flats in Utah. It was my heart that was racing when Joan told

June 13, 1953: Joan and I are married in a double-ring ceremony with her sister, Lenora, and my good friend, Don Fair.

me that she loved me, too. She accepted my slightly used fraternity pin and was soon making regular visits to the OSC campus in Corvallis for social events.

On Christmas Eve 1952, while at the Zemke home for their family celebration, I asked her father for Joan's hand in marriage. He gave his approval, and later that night, Joan accepted my proposal. On June 13, 1953—exactly one year and eleven days after our first date—we were married in a double-ring ceremony alongside Don and Lenora, who had become engaged on the very same night we had.

If the good Lord had told me on my wedding day that Joan and I would have one week short of sixty years together as husband and wife, I would have thought that was a pretty good deal. But not a day has gone by since Joan passed away in her sleep on June 5, 2013, when I haven't thought that fifty-nine years and fifty-one weeks at her side were not nearly enough.

Our children and grandchildren are an unending source
of pride and joy.

She was, quite simply, the most remarkable person I ever knew. She treated every individual with fairness, integrity, and honesty. If you wanted something done and done right, there was no one else in the world you would want in charge. A woman for all seasons, she assumed many roles in her life and filled them with perfection.

As a wife, she put up with my faults, always believing in me and helping me find the right course when, early in our marriage, I couldn't keep a job and when, later in our marriage, I couldn't keep away from alcohol.

As a mother, she did the lion's share of work in raising a son and a daughter who grew into outstanding, successful individuals who blessed us with five grandchildren she loved—and who loved her—more than I can say.

The biggest blessing of my life—my family. This photo was taken on Mother's Day 2012.

As a businesswoman, it was her intelligence and integrity that were front and center every day as we worked together to start and build a business from scratch—a business that today employs over one thousand people with annual sales of over three hundred million dollars. And it was her vision, creativity and persistence in the face of many doubters—myself included—that transformed a Yamhill County hillside into one of America's finest resorts—the Allison Inn & Spa.

And, as a philanthropist, it was her endless generosity that has immeasurably improved our community of Newberg, helped those in need, and ensured that countless nonprofit organizations could fulfill their missions.

Over the years, many friends and colleagues urged Joan and me to write a book that would share our personal story and

The A-dec complex in Newberg. What started in a twenty-five-by-forty-foot Quonset hut now occupies fifteen buildings on a fifty-acre campus.

how A-dec became the success it is. We never got around to doing it, perhaps because there were far more important things to do than talk or write about ourselves. I am blessed that family, friends, business, and philanthropy continue to keep my life busy, but as countless individuals have told me how much they loved and admired Joan, I concluded it was time to share the story of our journey together. What follows is not a detailed analysis of each and every innovation that was important to A-dec's success—I don't think even a dentist would want to read that! Rather, it is a collection of memories, stories, and lessons learned. I am well aware that writing this book won't bring Joan back, but it is my hope that those reading it will be inspired to live life as she did—with grace, with love, and with a servant's heart.

CHAPTER 1

AUSTIN FAMILY HERITAGE

Although I was born in Montana, there was never a doubt that Oregon was my home. Indeed, it was 1859—the same year Oregon became the thirty-third state in the union—when twenty-six-year-old Joshua Eberhard—my great-grandfather—arrived in Oregon's Willamette Valley. He had first traveled west from his native Ohio in 1855, arriving in San Francisco, California, with a widowed aunt and her two children. Four years later, at the urging of a relative who had written letters boasting about the high quality of farming in the small pioneer settlement of Butteville, they made their way north to Oregon.

Joshua found work in a local blacksmith shop and then purchased 720 acres of land that was once the site of John Jacob Astor's Willamette Post, a small trading settlement first established in 1812 by employees of the Pacific Fur Company. The only remnant of the Post was the chief trader's house, a twelve-by-twelve-foot dwelling that stood one and a half stories high, which Joshua used as his home.

The home was located approximately three hundred yards from the south bank of the Willamette River, a fact that led to disaster in 1860, when the worst flood in a century washed away nearly everything in its path. In a race against time, Joshua quickly assembled a team of horses to pull the house to

My dad and our dinner for that night!

higher ground before the floodwaters hit. He lost the chimney and fireplace, but he saved the mantel, which had traveled around the Cape Horn on a schooner and held much sentimental value.

In 1865, Joshua married Louisa Jones, the eldest daughter of his next-door neighbor. Together, they raised five sons and a daughter in a house that Joshua built himself and that still stands today. In 1891, Joshua's daughter, Barbara, then a twenty-three-year-old schoolteacher, married Henry Austin, a thirty-seven-year-old widower, who had moved fifteen years earlier from Iowa to the Quaker farm community of Newberg. They lived on the Eberhard family farm, and their marriage produced a daughter, Louise, and a son, George, who would become my father.

Dad was just sixteen years old when his father died in 1912. Along with his mother and sister, Dad moved from their farmhouse to Albany, Oregon, some fifty miles away, where he began his freshman year of high school. His school days did not last long. In his sophomore year, Dad lied about his age and joined the United States Coast Guard, stationed in a coastal artillery unit at Fort Stevens, near Astoria, Oregon.

When the United States declared war on Germany in 1917, Dad requested and received a discharge from the Coast Guard and went straight into the army, where he spent the next two years as an artilleryman in France with General Pershing's American Expeditionary Force.

Dad survived the war and returned home to Albany, where, at the age of twenty-two, he completed high school and then enrolled in nearby Albany College. To finance his education, he milked cows and competed at billiards, often beating the best players in town. He eventually graduated with a degree in

*My dad and his sister, Louise. Dad was
very proud of his service in World War I.*

accounting and found employment as a company clerk and
business manager for Shell Oil Company.

Dad was working for Shell in Walla Walla, Washington,
where, in the summer of 1925, he met Helen Van Winkle, a
beautiful and vivacious registered nurse. Following a six-month
whirlwind romance, they were married on December 6, 1925.
After brief assignments in Yakima and Seattle, Shell promoted
Dad to an office manager position in Missoula, Montana,
where I was born on October 29, 1931.

I have no memories of my time in Montana, as I was just
two years old when Shell told Dad that the division's head
office was being moved to Salt Lake City. I also have no

memories of the time we were in Salt Lake City, since we lived there for just a few months. Mom and Dad took an immediate disliking to the snowy Utah winter and to the smoke and soot that spewed out of the crude oil furnaces many residents used to keep warm.

Of more concern, however, was the news contained in letters from Dad's mother, who, since the death of her husband, had remained in Albany, while renting out the family farm. She depended on a local banker to collect the rent from the tenants, but when the Depression hit, it was hard to find anyone who could actually afford to pay the rent. The farmhouse was soon in disrepair, and the property became an eyesore. New tenants would promise to spruce it up, but they never did. As renters moved out, strangers came by and took what they wanted. Soon, someone began using the property to make and sell moonshine.

After hearing this news, my parents discussed how they could help. Mom suggested that Dad ask Shell for a transfer to the Oregon office in Portland. Such a move would put them just a half-hour's drive away from Newberg and perhaps allow them to get the farm ready to sell.

Dad had never considered himself a farmer, believing that the hard work required to make a living from a farm had contributed to the early death of his father. That is why it was such a surprise to Mom when Dad announced that he was quitting his job and we were moving to Oregon to live on the farm and to restore it to what it once used to be. We arrived in Newberg on February 17, 1934. It would be the last move of my parents' lives.

Joan's parents—Herman and Esther Zemke—were Minnesota farmers before moving to Oregon.

CHAPTER 2

ZEMKE FAMILY HERITAGE

For much of the last half the nineteenth century, German immigrants outnumbered every other immigrant nationality in the state of Minnesota. Included in this wave were Daniel Friedrich Wilhelm Zemke, his wife, Dorthea, and their seven children. Their eldest son, John, and his wife, Minnie, eventually had nine children, the seventh of which was named Herman. Born in 1904, Herman later married Esther Lachelt, and they were blessed with two sons and three daughters. The second eldest of their children was named Joan, and she would become the love of my life.

Born September 25, 1931, Joan spent her first ten years on the Zemke family farm near the tiny southwestern Minnesota community of Grove Lake. Home to only a few hundred people, Grove Lake consisted of a dry goods store, a community center, a filling station, a creamery, and a blacksmith shop.

Joan's father worked the land and raised grain, corn, cows, sheep, and pigs. Her mom managed the affairs of the house, which, with five children, was more than a full-time job. When the work was done, the family would relax by playing family card games or pitching horseshoes. If there was a Saturday night dance at the community center, Joan's parents would turn the event into an excursion for the entire family. In winter, Joan and her brothers and sisters would use a big shovel as a

Joan with an early pet. She would love animals her entire life.

makeshift sled and take turns using it to pull each other around a nearby frozen pond.

Joan often spoke of the generosity of her parents. Even though their farm barely broke even, they would reach out to those who were worse off and would help raise funds for worthy causes. Joan's mom was always preparing cakes and pies for barn raisings and church bake sales, and her parents provided a room to a local schoolteacher in need of a place to stay. This also allowed for the added benefit of having school right at home during winter blizzards.

Joan's strong work ethic began at a very young age. When her elder sister, Darlene, reached school age, she was afraid to go by herself. Wanting to give Darlene time to become accustomed to school, the Zemkes arranged for then four-year-old Joan to accompany Darlene for the first week of class. Joan worked hard to keep up with the other students, and when the week was done, the teacher said that Joan was doing very well and she should just continue coming to school.

Farming was as challenging in Minnesota as it was in Oregon, but the Zemkes persevered until the summer of 1941, when a severe storm destroyed that year's wheat crop. When the weather cleared, Joan's father drove the entire family out to survey the damage and announced that they were moving. After selling the farm and nonessential items at auction, all seven family members jammed into a four-door Nash sedan and set out for Oregon's Yamhill County, where Herman's sister lived. She had sent word that Oregon was a "land of plenty."

The family eventually settled in Newberg, from where Herman commuted to Portland after he found work as a millwright at a Portland company that manufactured doors and windows. Esther helped make ends meet by working in one of the many food processing plants found in the fertile agricultural region. Joan and her siblings also pitched in, working every summer in the strawberry and bean fields.

Joan always excelled in school, and if her family could have afforded it, she undoubtedly would have gone on to college. Money was tight, however, and she accepted a job at the home office of the Northwestern Mutual Fire Insurance Company in Portland. Her boss quickly grasped Joan's intelligence and abilities, and he served as a mentor as she learned every aspect of the insurance business over the course of several years. Part of his plan was to have her run her own agency, and, thankfully, he asked her to return to Newberg to get some management experience at an agency there. Had she remained in Portland or gone to an agency somewhere else, we might not have crossed paths again, and my life would have been immeasurably poorer.

CHAPTER 3

LIFE ON THE FARM

Anyone who has ever been a farmer knows that it takes a tremendous amount of hard work and dedication to succeed. Thankfully, my parents had an inexhaustible supply of both. From the very first day at the farm—when the broken farmhouse windows and a floor covered with nuts and leaves made it clear that my grandmother's letters had not overstated the severity of the situation—Dad and Mom rolled up their sleeves and went to work.

The main crops of the farm were wheat, oats, and grass for hay, and Dad soon set about clearing some bottomland by the river so he could also grow alfalfa. We had chickens for eggs, pigs for bacon and ham, and a cow for milk. Smart enough to know what he didn't know, Dad was an avid reader of *Oregon Farmer* magazine and bulletins published by the Oregon State College Extension Service, and he also sought the advice of the local OSC agriculture extension agents. As he purchased more cows, he joined the Dairy Herd Improvement Association, which kept members up-to-date on how best to achieve maximum yields of butterfat. He also became one of the first farmers in the area to irrigate his land, which gave him better hay crops from fresh new soil. The irrigation also made the farm ideal for clover, which translated into some of the best milk and cream in the Willamette Valley. If I drank a glass of

The Austin family farm outside of Newberg. To grow up on a farm is to never be bored.

milk from our farm and one from another farm, I could tell you which was which. I wasn't the only one who could taste the difference, as the creamery that Dad used often sold his product exclusively to VIP customers.

While I went to the local public schools once I was old enough, my true education occurred on our farm. To be a kid growing up on a farm means never being bored. There was always a task that needed to be done, a chore to be accomplished, or a new adventure to begin. It was no wonder my mother always claimed she had difficulty in getting me to take a nap! My companion through it all was my father. Indeed, as an only child with my school classmates living more than a mile away, Dad quickly became my best buddy. My earliest memories involve crawling up on the seat of Dad's Model A Ford truck and setting out with him for a busy day of chores.

There were oats to be harvested with a horse-drawn grain binder. There were cows to be milked—including the one that

gave me a swift kick when I ignored Dad's warning and ventured too close to her hind legs, teaching me a lesson I never forgot. There was land to be cleared and stumps to be dynamited out of the ground. There were cans of cream to haul on my little red wagon out to where they could be picked up by the local creamery. There was a log cabin to be built in the woods across the road from our house, where I pretended to be a pioneer. Above all, there were trucks and tractors and machinery to fix and maintain.

My lifelong passion of building and fixing and tinkering with all things mechanical began when I was five or six years old. As Dad and I went around the farm, I would ask him, "What are they doing out there?" He would answer that they were pounding out a plowshare in the blacksmith shop, or they were welding, or they were rewinding a motor, or they were building a hoist for a tractor. It was an easy step to go from watching someone fix or build a piece of equipment to wanting to fix or build it myself. I was very fortunate that Dad was a great teacher. If I wanted to do something, he would help me. If I needed a piece of steel, he would get it for me. When I was seven, he gave me an old Maytag washing machine motor and worked with me to get it started. When we finally got it to run, I had great visions of using it to power a go-cart. That never happened, but I did learn enough about ignition systems and carburetion to fix a three-horsepower engine with a buzz saw attached.

Another early influence on my fascination with mechanics was Russell Landfare, a turkey farmer who lived alone down the road from us. Russell was always working on something, and he usually asked me to help out. He had lots of tools, demonstrated how to use them, and even gave me ones he no longer needed but knew I would enjoy. He taught me the workings of a thermostat, showed me how to build a windmill and let me help him build a sawmill. I've often thought you could divide people into two groups—doers and stewers. Russell was a doer, and my friendship with him introduced me to things other kids never got a chance to do.

When I wasn't following Dad around or tinkering with something mechanical, I could probably be found in the kitchen, where Mom or my Dad's mother and sister—who moved from Albany back to the farm and lived with us for a number of years—were cooking up something delicious. I was fortunate to have three moms growing up—my mother, Grandma Austin, and Aunt Louise. When I returned home in the afternoons from school, I could tell—or *smell*—that Grandma had been busy. "I've got something for you," she would say as she spread cream and brown sugar on freshly baked bread.

I was fortunate to grow up in a close family. Pictured here are my father, my grandmother, my Aunt Louise, and my mother—each of whom was a tremendous influence on my life.

As it did for all Americans, our world changed on December 7, 1941, when the Japanese attack on Pearl Harbor brought the United States into World War II. Everyone in the family and everyone we knew was somehow involved in the war effort. We conducted scrap metal drives and adopted a lifestyle based on rationing. Mom folded bandages for the American Red Cross, and as a devoted member of the American Legion Auxiliary, she saved and recycled tin foil, tin cans and old newspapers. She also joined the Oregon Air Watch, a group of citizen volunteers whose job it was to identify planes that flew over the area and estimate their height and speed. She put in two days a week peering at the sky through binoculars.

My cousin Bill and I standing in front of my first workshop.

Soon after the attack on Pearl Harbor, farmers around the country attended repair schools to learn how to keep their equipment operating without having access to new or spare parts, which were needed for the war effort. When Dad attended these classes at the local International Tractor dealer, he allowed me to tag along. We had an old outboard motor that wouldn't run, and Dad eventually brought it to one of the classes so the two of us could tinker with it. I'll never forget my excitement when we got that motor running! It was also about this time when I set up my first shop. I called it "The Boys Club," and I took on projects like building birdhouses and sharpening knives with an old hand grinder.

I began my freshman year at Newberg High School in September of 1945 and very much enjoyed my four years there. I participated in football, track and field, student council, and

My buddies and I working on my first car. I'm second from the left.

started the Camera Club, which initiated my lifelong interest in photography. (In fact, I still have my very first camera, a folding vest-pocket model Kodak 127 Hawkeye.) It was all things mechanical, however, that remained at the center of my high school years and to which I devoted most of my time.

The highlight of my freshman year was coming under the influence of Howard Bennett, the school's agriculture teacher. Mr. Bennett prepared students to be good farmers, and much to my delight, he also taught shop class, as he was an outstanding mechanic and welder. I couldn't wait to get to his class each day.

When I turned fourteen in October 1945, I passed the test to receive my student driver's permit, allowing me to drive the five miles from our farm to school. My transportation was a 1928 Chevrolet coupe bought from a neighbor with some of the money my dad paid me for the cows I had raised as a 4-H project. As you might imagine, the car needed some work, so I went shopping at a war surplus store and arrived home with a used electric welder, a welding outfit, a chain hoist, and a hydraulic jack. I used the equipment to tinker with my car and to help my buddies tinker with theirs. My best friend, Bruce Rummer, could usually be found at my side.

In July 1947, the summer before our junior year, we decided that more space was needed to work on cars and that we should build a shop between our house and the barn. After Bruce and I poured concrete for the foundation, we recruited friends to help put up the frame. My parents provided the lumber in exchange for my promise that I would add another forty feet to my dad's machine shed. (I still feel guilty that I never kept that promise.) When the building was finished, I painted a sign that proclaimed the opening of "The Rod Shop." That sign now hangs proudly in a garage that houses my antique car collection. The exact wording of it is: "The Rod Shop; Custom Work; Speed Equipment; PH3F12; Kenny Austin Jr." I can't even begin to estimate the number of hours I spent in the Rod Shop, elbow deep in car engines, but suffice to say that had I devoted the same time to studying for my classes, my grades would have been a whole lot better!

Another interest I developed during my teenage years was aviation. I loved driving fast in cars, and I imagined it might be even more fun to fly fast. My first ride in an airplane was courtesy of a local pilot named Sam Whitney. It was even more exciting than I had imagined, and I gave Sam some building materials we had at the farm in exchange for a series of flying lessons.

The original "Rod Shop" sign remains one of my most prized possessions.

I was very proud of the fact that Dad was a World War I veteran, and I joined with my family and the entire community of Newberg in saluting those who served in World War II. Soon after turning seventeen in December 1948, I made the decision to do my part for my country by joining the National Guard. Training for the Battery C Unit of the 218th Field Auxiliary was conducted in the basement of Newberg's American Legion Hall. The forty or so members of our unit would occasionally travel on weekends a few hours north in a convoy to Fort Lewis in the state of Washington, where we would practice our marksmanship on the firing range. A friend and I also thought it might be fun to volunteer to help the mess sergeant, where we ended up cracking more eggs than we could possibly count.

CHAPTER 4

COLLEGE DAYS

Despite my preference for socket wrenches over schoolbooks, I did manage to pass all my classes, and as my June 1949 high school graduation day approached, I spent time pondering my future. Many friends in classes above mine had not gone on to college and were making good money as electricians or in construction, and I gave serious thought to following them into the workforce. While telling me the decision was mine to make, Mom and Dad, who were both college graduates, made it clear that their strong preference was for me to continue with my education. Once I made the decision to do just that, the choice of which college to attend was an easy one. In the summer of 1945, I had been selected from my 4-H chapter to attend a weeklong summer school at Oregon State College in Corvallis. I had the time of my life and was greatly impressed by the size and beauty of the campus. I knew then that if college was in my future, OSC would be that college.

I arrived on campus in the fall of 1949, and the same study habits—or lack of them—I exhibited in high school unfortunately carried over to my freshman year at OSC. While I did well in my mechanical drawing class, I quickly fell behind in courses like English and Algebra. Rather than devoting more time to studying for those classes, I unwisely threw

Subject	Crs.	No.	Hrs.	Gr.	Pts.
Engr Drawing		111	2	B	6
English	Eng	X	1	F	—
Inter Algebra	Mth	100	4	C	8
Extempore Speak	Speak	111	3	d	6
Gen Hygiene	PE	150	1	C	2
Naval Orient	NS	111	3	F	—
Amer Natl Govt	PS	201	3	F	—
Totals			17		22

GRADE REPORT

Name Austin, George Kenneth School Engr Class Fresh Term Fall 19 49-50

Mr. Geo. K. Austin
Rt. 1
AURORA, OREGON

GPA 1.29

NAVY

Office of the Registrar, Oregon State College

My first term college GPA was an embarrassing 1.29! Thanks to some professors who took an interest in me, I soon got my act together.

myself into a busy social life. I especially enjoyed helping out with the homecoming bonfire and parade. I was appointed equipment chairman for the bonfire, which meant spending the better part of a week hauling wood and scrap from all over Corvallis. Parade participants were challenged to build the float that made the loudest noise, and I succeeded by borrowing the City of Newberg's official air-raid siren and hitching it to a trailer. The more I did outside the classroom, the further I fell behind inside the classroom. When the first-term grades arrived in January 1950, I was close to flunking out, with a grade point average of only 1.29.

My reaction to receiving these grades was to be one of the turning points in my life. My initial thought was that the bad grades were a sign I was not cut out for college, and it was time to find a job or join the military. And truth be told, I did come very close to dropping out. But something inside of me did not want to admit failure. The night those first-semester grades were revealed, I promised myself that I would show everyone that I was better than those grades suggested. Moreover, I decided that night to prove my worth by building a hot rod with an engine and parts I would make myself.

Just as I had been blessed in high school with teachers who took an interest in me, there were also professors at OSC who were very influential in setting me on the right course. Had it not been for four gentlemen—Professor "Poppy" Popovich, who was dean of engineering; automotive engineering professor Bill Paul; Ed Meyers, a mechanical pattern making instructor; and George Cox, who gave me a set of keys to the engineering laboratory—I very well might not have graduated and certainly would not be where I am today. All four of these men became mentors, encouraging my interest in mechanics and engines and refusing to express skepticism or disdain when I advanced ideas that were not traditional or were not how it was covered in our textbooks. Not once did I hear any of these gentlemen say—as some of my other professors had—"What the heck are you thinking about, Austin?"

Their support and recommendations also helped me land a summer internship at Tekronix, a new Oregon high-tech company that manufactured measurement devices. I worked as a welder at Tektronix the summers after my freshman, sophomore, and junior years. The money I earned there helped me pay for my education, and the experience also cemented my interest in mechanics and industrial engineering. While there, I also had the good fortune of becoming acquainted with company cofounder Jack Murdock. Jack was kind enough to take an interest in me, and he patiently answered my questions and listened to my suggestions. He also sensed that I did not like taking orders, and he encouraged me to dream about running my own business. When A-dec was up and running, Jack continued to provide encouragement. His passing in a plane crash in 1971 was a great loss to his family and many friends. His influence has continued, however, through the generous gifts that the Murdock Charitable Trust has made to many nonprofit organizations in the Pacific Northwest.

Another mentor was Colonel Morris, who ran the campus Air Force ROTC program. (When I left Newberg for college, the National Guard granted me an honorable discharge, with the understanding that I would enroll in the ROTC program at OSC.) When I was thinking about dropping out and perhaps enlisting in the Air Force, Colonel Morris explained to me that if I enlisted without a college degree, I would enter as a lowly cadet, but if I stayed in college and received a diploma, I would qualify for pilot training as a commissioned officer.

Because of the professors who allowed me to follow my passions, my grades and my attitude steadily improved. In the spring term of my junior year, I decided to try out for OSC Yell King. The job of the Yell King was to encourage school spirit at football games and pep rallies. Famed OSC Athletic Director Spec Keene interviewed all the applicants, and I left my interview thinking the job was mine. Instead, Keene chose my good friend Bill Sunstrom. As we walked across campus after Keene announced his decision, Bill asked why I thought he had been chosen over me. Before I had a chance to answer, he said, "It's because I proposed to Spec that OSC have a mascot, and that you were the best person to do it."

"What the heck does a mascot do?" I blurted out. Bill explained that the job of a mascot was to "liven things up." Growing up, my family had attended local rodeos, and it dawned on me that the job of a mascot sounded a lot like the job of a rodeo clown. I told Bill my memories of rodeo clowns making people laugh and livening things up by using props like a toilet plunger and a gun that shot blanks. Bill listened, laughed, and told me the job was mine.

OSC sports teams were, of course, known as the Beavers, and with the help of a costume shop in Portland, Bill and I created a papier-mâché beaver head and tail and covered both with brown shag carpeting. We completed the look with shoulder pads, a jersey, football pants, and football shoes.

"Benny Beaver" made his debut on October 4, 1952, when OSC kicked off its football season against Michigan State at Multnomah Stadium (now Providence Park) in Portland. I put on my outfit in the locker room, and when the game began, I did everything possible to keep the crowd revved up and entertained. I made fun of the referees when they made a bad call. I shot blanks into the air when the Beavers scored. I used a plunger to beat on the bass drum when the marching band's drummer wasn't looking. I was nervous when the game started, but after getting my first laugh, I had the time of my life. I even shimmied up the opposing team's goalpost to create a distraction, and stayed there until the play moved closer to the end zone or until the referee yelled at me to get down or risk an unsportsmanlike conduct penalty. Benny continued his act at all that season's home football games and at away games at Stanford and Washington State University.

When the 1952 football season ended that November, popular demand called for Benny to repeat his act during the Beaver basketball season. It took only one basketball game, however, for me to conclude that the confines of an indoor gymnasium didn't allow for the same antics as an outdoor

*One of the highlights of my college years—serving
as the first "Benny Beaver."*

football field—especially using a gun to shoot blanks—and my
time as Benny ended quickly. Sixty years later, Benny is a
regular at almost every Beaver athletic contest, and I remain
"dam" proud of the role I played in bringing him to life

CHAPTER 5

MARRIED LIFE AND MILITARY LIFE

As I look back at my years at OSC, many of my favorite memories involve Joan. We began dating in the summer of 1952, and when I returned to Corvallis that fall, Joan would frequently join me for football games, dances, and social activities. It was no surprise that my friends quickly fell in love with her. When we couldn't be together, I burned up the phone line, sharing with her what had happened in my classes and the latest news from campus.

After our June 1953 wedding and a honeymoon in Victoria, British Columbia, Joan and I spent the first few months as husband and wife in a small one-bedroom apartment in Newberg. When the school year began in September, we moved to an even smaller apartment near the OSC campus in Corvallis, where I would complete the two terms of credits necessary to obtain my college diploma. With business experience and plenty of in-demand office skills, Joan was quickly able to find a job as the secretary to the dean of the Department of Animal Husbandry. Joan fell in love with all things OSC, and one of the joys of our sixty years together was our passion for making Oregon State University a world-class institution.

My fascination with aviation would lead me to fly for Uncle Sam.

May 1954 was to be a life-changing month for Joan and me. It began on May 1, with the birth of our son, Ken III. Then, on May 14, I received my Air Force commission and my orders to begin my commitment to the military by reporting for basic officer's training at Lackland Air Force Base near San Antonio, Texas. Joined by our new son, Joan and I soon began the long drive to Texas, preventing me from personally receiving my Industrial Administration degree at OSC commencement ceremonies that June.

Our time in San Antonio was short as I was quickly assigned to undergo flight training at Columbus Air Base in Columbus, Mississippi. We were fortunate to find housing on the first floor of a beautiful southern home owned by a wonderful older couple who treated us like family. My days were filled by learning everything there was to know about the Piper Cub and the T-6 Texan, the two small single-engine airplanes in which I received my training.

My flight instructor was "Papa" Kerns, who was known as the best and the toughest instructor in the squadron, and my final flight before I would be allowed to solo was one that I will never forget. Kerns was sitting behind me as I piloted the plane to six thousand feet. Everything seemed normal as I leveled off and switched fuel tanks. Kerns asked me to take the plane into a controlled spin, and I did as instructed. Without warning, he grabbed the controls from me and put the plane in a much faster and steeper spin. He then turned the controls over to me, yelling that I was a stupid pilot and if I couldn't control the plane, I was through. I managed to make what I thought was an expert recovery and guided the plane out of the spin. Kerns was unimpressed, telling me that I was the worst student he had ever had and predicting that I would spin my plane into the ground one day and it would be his job to tell Joan what had happened and to listen to Ken III ask, "Where's my Daddy?" He continued to berate me throughout the entire flight, and after I executed what I thought was a very successful landing, he climbed out of the plane and simply said, "See if you can land it solo without killing yourself."

Thoughts of quitting raced through my mind, but I quickly resolved to prove to him that I could fly better than any of my classmates. It was only after talking to those classmates that I realized some of them had also received the same treatment during their solo flight. Training the "Kerns way" was designed to weed out pilots who could not remain calm during a time of great stress and pressure. Of the eighty pilots who began flight

I loved flying the T-33 at Webb Air Force Base in Big Springs, Texas.

training with me, half successfully finished and half washed out.

From Mississippi, it was back to Texas and Webb Air Force Base near Big Springs for training in the single engine T-28 and the jet-propelled T-33. I was awarded my pilot's wings on July 18, 1955, and received orders informing me that I would be stationed in South Korea after completing a three-month assignment at Radar Controller School at Tyndal Air Force Base in Panama City, Florida.

When that training was completed in October 1955, I used furlough time to drive Joan and Kenny from Florida back to Newberg. Dependent travel was not allowed for my Korean assignment, so we wanted some time together before we were separated as a family for the first time. We began the trip by touring the East Coast and visiting places we had always wanted to visit, including New York City and Niagara Falls. We also planned a stop in Washington, DC, so I could drop by the Pentagon to tell someone my hope that my time at Radar Controller School didn't mean I would spend my time in Korea staring at a radar scope. My preference, of course, was to use the training I had received and to actually work as a pilot. If that couldn't occur, then I planned on suggesting they give me an assignment that would enable me to use my mechanical and engineering experience.

Upon arriving at the Pentagon, I went directly to the Officer Classification unit, where I told the sergeant at the front desk that I wanted to talk to someone about being mal-assigned. "Those are pretty harsh words, Lieutenant," he warned. We were soon joined by another sergeant, and then by a major. As I detailed my entire resume, I could see they were actually listening to me and believed that I was making sense. The major told me that while he couldn't take me out of the overseas allotment for Air Force aircraft controllers, he encouraged me to keep telling my story and said his guess was that I would eventually be assigned to a job that matched my passion and talents.

Taking his advice to heart, I presented my case to anyone who would listen during a brief layover in Japan and told it again upon landing in South Korea. There, one officer asked if I knew anything about diesel engines, as he needed someone to look after the generators that powered the radar at base K-6 in Pyeongtaek. I told him the truth—that base K-6 was the base where I had been ordered to report, and that I was very well acquainted with diesel engines. My assignment was changed on the spot, and I learned a valuable lesson about the importance of not being afraid to sell myself.

Base K-6, my home for my eleven-month Korean assignment, looked like a war zone—which it had been during the Korean War that had ended just two years earlier. I very much missed Joan and Kenny, and I decided the way to make time go quicker was to stay busy. I worked most of the time, and rather than moping in my Quonset hut, I spent my spare time talking and eating with my fellow officers. When my time in Korea was finally over, I arranged for Joan to meet me in Hawaii for a second honeymoon, thinking we might never get there again. We stayed for five days at the beautiful Hawaiian Village Hotel for the military rate of fourteen dollars a night.

When our vacation was over, I went to Hickam Field to coordinate the departure of my military flight with Joan's commercial flight so we would arrive in San Francisco at the same time. From there, we had reservations to take the train back to Portland, where we would spend some additional furlough time before I had to report to Myrtle Beach, South Carolina, for an assignment as an aircraft maintenance officer. Imagine my delight when I recognized the transportation officer at Hickam as a friend of mine from pilot training class in Mississippi. He made all the arrangements for Joan to fly back to the mainland with me on C-97 Stratofreighter troop and cargo carrier. Having seats in the VIP section helped to make it an unforgettable ending to a very special week.

Joan and Ken III joined me in Myrtle Beach during my assignment there from November 1956 to June 1957. When that assignment was complete, so, too, was my ROTC commitment to the military. My superiors in Myrtle Beach tried talking me into extending my service for two additional years and even offered me a flying assignment. Joan and I talked it over, and we both agreed it was time to return home to Oregon.

CHAPTER 6

SIX JOBS IN FIVE YEARS

As Joan and I and three-year-old Kenny left Myrtle Beach in June 1957, we headed north again to enjoy sights we had missed on our first trip up the East Coast two years earlier. Pulling a one-wheel trailer, we drove to New York City to see the Statue of Liberty, and then headed west for Yellowstone National Park. During the long hours on the road, Joan and I dreamed about our future. We talked about where we would live and what we would do. We both agreed that Newberg was the logical place to make our home, as both sets of our parents could help with Ken III when we went to work. Joan mulled returning to an insurance agency, and I seriously considered buying a Newberg Shell service station, which also featured a fix-it shop. The owner, who was a friend of my father, was nearing retirement, and tinkering with everything from cars to lawnmowers to toasters seemed like something that might fit my skills. He eventually decided he wasn't quite ready to sell the station, but for the first time I felt that my destiny might be to go into business for myself.

When we arrived in Newberg, we quickly set about finding a home, and with money saved from my time in the military, we rented a house that was definitely a fixer-upper. I searched the want ads in newspapers, and an engineer's position at Powder Power Tool caught my eye. When I went in for an initial interview with a manager, I was asked, "What do you want to be doing in ten years?" I answered, "Have my own business." With that response, I flunked the interview. The manager told me they were looking for employees who would be loyal to the company, and that I should never tell prospective employers that I wanted to go into business for myself.

I next interviewed at Morrow Radio, a Salem, Oregon, company that built navigational radios and was an affiliate of Tektronix. I didn't get the job, but it did spur me to apply directly to Tektronix, where I contacted the individual who had interviewed me for my college internship there. This contact paid off, as I was hired as a mechanical design engineer with the responsibilities of making parts for oscilloscopes (an instrument used to detect the change in electrical currents) and designing and making the tools necessary to build the parts.

The job paid $330 a month, and I showed up for work thinking I was pretty hot stuff. The military had allowed me to have some fascinating experiences and to live in some interesting places. The people I worked with were talented tool and die makers, but since most had not attended college and not traveled anywhere, I assumed we had little in common. Instead of actually getting to know them, I spent my time hanging out with electrical engineers in other departments, oblivious to the fact that my actions caused my coworkers to correctly conclude that I thought I was too good for them. They made their feelings known to my boss and when, after three months on the job, I went to him to ask about my future in the company, he said, "It's funny you should ask," he began, and then added, "Maybe you should look for work elsewhere."

I was in the job market again, and after a few leads and interviews didn't pan out, I made my way to Corvallis to visit with Bill Paul, my favorite mechanical engineering professor. Bill had great contacts with many of Portland's top manufacturing businesses, and I asked him if he knew of any companies that would fit my automotive interests. He passed along a couple of leads, which eventually led to my being hired by P&G Supply, a business that bought surplus government-owned diesel engines and converted them to civilian use for tug, fishing, and pleasure boats, as well as selling automotive equipment. My job would be driving around in a pickup truck looking for buyers of that equipment. With an agreement that my salary would be $330 net a month, I went to work and made a number of good sales.

When my first payday arrived after two weeks on the job, I was surprised that my salary was $330 a month gross, and that with all the taxes being withheld from my paycheck, I was only making $230 a month net. My boss refused to raise my salary, and he gave me the distinct impression that he saw me as nothing more than a temporary hire he would just keep around for a few projects.

Wanting to prove I was worthy of continued employment and a raise, I told my boss that I had a solution to a problem he was wrestling with. The surplus military engines he was buying came equipped with military oil filters, which were bigger than commercial filters. My boss wanted the military filters, which were bolted to the engine block, replaced with standard filters, and I devised a new casting that would make that possible. I made the pattern in my shop and took it to the Oregon City Foundry, which I had used for casting on some of my automotive projects during college, and arranged for them to make the part. Certain that I was now worth more to the company, I asked again for a raise. Instead, I was fired after just three months on the job.

My reconnection with the Oregon City Foundry led me to ask that company's owner if I could make patterns and work in the machine shop. He called me a few days later to offer me a sales job instead. For two months, I did all I could to attract business to the company and had very little success. I did, however, learn a very valuable lesson that would be at the core of my philosophy when I did begin my own business: if you want to take business away from somebody, you have to provide a better product, better service, and better quality at a better price. The Oregon City Foundry, while a reputable and professional business, simply had nothing unique to offer.

Realizing that I was struggling, the owner agreed to transfer me to the machine shop, where I would produce metal parts. It was around this time that I also joined the Air Force Reserve as a pilot. Once a month, I flew the C-119 Flying Boxcar cargo planes out of Portland, giving me some additional income. That income became even more of a priority in November 1958, when the arrival of our daughter, Loni, completed our family. A few weeks later, I left the foundry when an old friend told me that his manufacturing company in Portland had just received a contract from Boeing to design a seat for a space vehicle, and he asked me to join his team as a draftsman.

This was my fourth job in a little over a year, and it initially seemed that I had finally found a good fit. My salary was good, the work was challenging and interesting, and almost before I knew it, I had been at the same job for nearly two years. As time went on, I became increasingly upset with certain working conditions, including the fact that the facility was dirty and cold with very poor ventilation. Trouble developed when we got behind on a project and my supervisor asked me to work a few Saturdays. I was scheduled on Air Force Reserve duty those days and preferred flying to working, so I simply didn't answer his request. A few days later, I was told to come get my toolbox, and I was back on the rolls of the unemployed.

The old saying "It's not what you know, it's who you know" came into play again when I called Harry Everett, an old friend I had bumped into in the course of my last job, who had told me to check with him if I were ever on the market again. Harry ran the new product division at a business called Power Brake Equipment, and he offered me a job in his three-man department.

I began at PBE shortly after Labor Day 1960 and was excited to learn that my first assignment was to design valves for the air brake department. It was an assignment that allowed me to use the skills gained in college and my lifelong interest in all things automotive, and I threw myself into the work. Three months into my project, PBE landed a contract from the United States Air Force to build twenty portable dental units that could fit in a suitcase, and I was asked to head operations on the contract. While I knew that PBE had a dental product division, I never imagined working there. In fact, I hated going to the dentist, and it was hard to imagine anything duller than manufacturing dental equipment. I dragged my feet for two weeks, hoping my boss might offer the job to someone else. My hopes were dashed when he delivered an ultimatum that I either accepted the transfer or I was fired. Had he not given me that ultimatum, A-dec might never have existed.

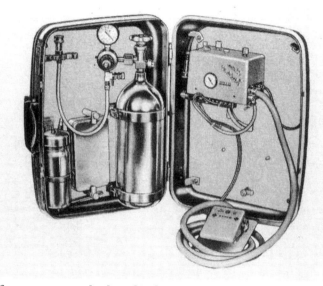

*My first exposure to the dental industry was at Williams Air Controls,
where I developed a dental travel kit for military use.*

Contrary to my initial beliefs, designing and manufacturing
dental equipment was interesting and challenging work. I
would remain in the dental unit for nearly three years, and I
was proud of the role I played in helping the department grow
from three employees to more than sixty. (One of those
employees was Joan, who worked in clerical support.) It was at
PBE where I would learn the fundamentals of air valves and
air controls, and it was there that I became acquainted with the
concept of a field dental unit, which packaged dental equipment
in a portable container. It was there that I would learn to focus
on the needs of customers and to design products that were
simple and easy to maintain. All of these were lessons that
would eventually be instrumental in the formation and success
of A-dec. It was also there that, after a disagreement over
company procedures, I found myself fired yet again.

Thankfully, I soon learned of an opening in the engineering department of Densco, a dental equipment company based in Denver, Colorado. I thought my three years of experience at PBE provided me with the necessary qualifications, and Joan encouraged me to apply, saying she would be willing to move our family to Colorado. The only problem was that I needed to get to Denver for an interview, and I couldn't afford a plane ticket. A solution appeared when Louise Sullivan, one of my former managers at PBE, told me they were thinking of buying a company in Los Angeles, and she asked if I would fly to California on PBE's dime to review the company and report back to her. I told her I would be happy to take on the assignment, but only if they provided me with a plane ticket that would take me from Portland to Los Angeles to Denver and back. She agreed, and a few days later, on November 1, 1963, I was hired at Densco as the new chief engineer, with a two-year contract that paid me what I regarded as the princely sum of eighteen thousand dollars a year. Joan organized the move with her usual efficiency, and within a few weeks, we had packed up the house and the kids and set out for a new life in Colorado. We quickly bought a split-level ranch-style home in the Denver suburb of Broomfield and joined the local country club, and I thought we had it made. I was wrong.

CHAPTER 7

BREAD AND BEANS

Before reporting to work at Densco, I had made a list of possible new products for the company. Company executives were sufficiently impressed to agree to my request for a contract awarding me a 10 percent royalty on the sales of any product on my list that they developed and sold. I thought this contract elevated me above my coworkers. In my mind, I was the company president's fair-haired boy, and I made sure everyone knew it. It didn't take long for the eight people I worked with to get sick of me. They went to the company president and said that he needed to fire me or they were all quitting. I compounded the problem by taking a week-long vacation without asking for approval. On my first day at the office after the vacation, I was summoned to the executive suite and told to be out of my office by noon.

I was in job-hunting mode once again and called several vendors I had worked with at Densco. Nothing panned out—perhaps because I had foolishly listed Densco as a reference, and when prospective employers called, they didn't give me the most glowing of recommendations. Thinking I'd had my fill of engineering jobs, I went to United Airlines to see if they needed pilots, only to learn that at age thirty-two, I was two years past the maximum age limit for new pilots. Approaching desperation and needing to make our monthly mortgage payment, I applied with Kelly Temporary Services. When a company needed a draftsman for a short-term assignment, Kelly would provide temporary "rent-a-pencils." Learning that they might soon have an assignment for me was the best news Joan and I had heard in several weeks, and we decided to take the kids on a picnic to celebrate. It was to be a picnic that would change our lives.

It was Sunday, September 20, 1964, and the view from Red Rocks State Park outside of Denver was breathtaking. As we watched Ken III and Loni play, I shared with Joan an idea that I had been mulling over. One of the many products manufactured by Densco was an oral evacuation system. This system was made necessary by the invention of the high-speed air drill in the 1950s, which created a need for a device that would clean debris from a patient's mouth fast enough to keep the working area clean so the dentist could continue drilling. I had heard from a number of dentists that the Densco system, which was similar to systems manufactured by other dental equipment companies, was difficult to hold, as it required a large, motor-driven vacuum. I had been tinkering in my head with the design of a new evacuator that would be more compact and more efficient. I explained that to Joan and concluded by telling her that two former employees of Densco had recently gone on to start their own business. I wondered out loud that if they could start a business, why couldn't we do it, too? Her response came quickly and has forever remained in my memory. She said, "If you want to do that, I will help you, even if we have to live on bread and beans." Is it any wonder why I loved her so much?

While we had been able to build a modest savings account, we knew it wouldn't last long without a regular salary coming in. Experienced draftsmen were rarely out of work in a growing city like Denver, and I was confident that Kelly would be calling with temporary jobs. I also knew that accepting those assignments would take me away from my most pressing task—developing a more efficient, more reliable, and less expensive oral evacuator. So as soon as we arrived home, I went to the couch in our living room, pulled out some sketching paper, and got to work.

By bedtime that evening, my sketch was complete. I called Kelly the next morning to tell them that I wouldn't be accepting any assignments for the time being and set out to find a machine shop where I could build and test a prototype of what Ken III and Loni had promptly nicknamed my "super slobber sucker." (Ken III would also be the one to propose Austin Dental Equipment Company—or A-dec—as the name of our new business.)

After a few initial rejections, I was able find a shop that agreed to lease space to me for a dollar a day. Two days later, a prototype was ready for testing. I loaded nine-year-old Ken III into the car and headed for a nearby service station, where I made two requests: could I hook up my invention to their air supply, and could I have a bucket of water? If my evacuator system could suck water out of the bucket, I knew it would be a success. When it performed beyond my wildest dreams, you could hear my yell of "It works! It works!" across the Rockies.

The next step was to demonstrate my invention to potential customers, and I traveled to Oregon to take advantage of my contacts and connections there. By the time I arrived, I had developed a serious case of cold feet. While meeting with Louise Sullivan, who had been one of my bosses at PBE, I suddenly asked for my old job back, offering to sell ownership of my new vacuum system to PBE in exchange for a salary plus a 10 percent royalty. My proposal rightfully confused her. "On the one hand you want to work for me," she said. "And on the other hand you seem excited about starting your own business. You can't have both." She told me to think about it overnight and to return the next morning with my answer.

As I mulled my decision that evening, I reflected on my checkered employment career. Since my military commitment had ended in 1957, I had held six jobs, and essentially been fired six times. In each instance, I had courted trouble by suggesting what I thought was a better way to do something. The problem was that wasn't my job. It became clear to me that if I wanted to have the authority to fix something I thought needed fixing, then I needed to be the boss. I called Joan that evening to share my thoughts and to seek her wise counsel, and her encouraging words removed any last vestiges of self-doubt. When I arrived back at Louise's office, I told her that Joan and I would be starting our own business, and that we had one request. If our business was to have a chance at success, we needed a list of possible customers, and I knew that Louise had a Rolodex that included all the companies that purchased dental products from PBE. She graciously agreed, allowing me to take her Rolodex back to Denver, where Joan painstakingly copied her list of names, addresses, and phone numbers on a pile of three-by-five index cards and filed them in a recipe box. When she was finished, we had about 150 names of trustworthy businesses that might be interested in our new evacuation system.

We knew that many of those customers would be attending the annual American Dental Association convention, which would soon convene in San Francisco and offer a prime opportunity to show my oral evacuator prototype to the biggest and best companies in the industry, including the S.S. White Company, which, at the time, was the nation's largest dental equipment manufacturer and retailer. Before leaving for the convention, Joan and I worked with a printing company in Denver to produce some promotional material, which included our company name, address, and a price list. This information was printed on a small strip of paper that could be rolled up and inserted into the opening in the plastic tip of the evacuator. The tip was actually another product I had recently developed. The tips attached to other evacuators on the market were made of metal and had to undergo a time-consuming sterilization process after each use. The tips on my evacuator were made of very light plastic and were meant to be disposed of after each use. The tips cost two cents apiece to make, and I brought some samples with me to California. My plan was to give these tips away as samples, with the hope that if they liked the sample, they would buy some more.

With the prototype evacuator carefully tucked away in my briefcase, I flew to San Francisco on November 7, 1964. The visit got off to a great start when executives from the dental equipment company Vacudent ordered twenty thousand tips at four cents apiece. Since they only cost me two cents apiece to make, I quickly calculated that A-dec was four hundred dollars in the black. The good news continued when I was able to arrange a meeting with three of the top S.S. White executives—a meeting that began in one of their hotel rooms and continued over breakfast. They examined my prototype from every angle, made a few suggestions for possible improvement, and declared that "if it works like you say it does, and if you can keep the cost at no more than eighty dollars a unit, then we want it."

Having the industry giant see the potential of my invention was tremendously exciting, as was the fact that on the flight to California I had penciled out the numbers on a napkin and knew the unit cost was well under eighty dollars. In fact, after reworking the evacuator to their specifications, I estimated A-dec's cost at around forty dollars a unit, and S.S. White agreed to pay me sixty dollars a unit—a tidy net profit.

Final approval of our agreement was contingent upon additional testing of the improved prototype, which I hand delivered to company executives in New York City soon after Thanksgiving 1964. What followed were three excruciating months of waiting. Joan and I had devoted a great deal of time and money in the courtship of S.S. White, and if they ended up saying thanks but no thanks, we would be approaching a financial disaster.

Never one to just sit and wait, Joan set up office at a small desk in our basement and telephoned potential customers from the index cards in her recipe box. She also called on a few banks in the Denver area to inquire about the possibility of getting a loan to tide our new business over in case of the worst-case scenario. The banks expressed some interest, but it was obvious that we would have to jump through an endless series of time-consuming hoops to receive a loan.

With our backs against the wall, we borrowed four hundred dollars against an insurance policy Joan had taken out right after high school, received a four-hundred-dollar line of credit from a Newberg bank, and my father loaned us another four hundred dollars. When a Newberg dentist, to whom I had demonstrated my evacuator when I was in Oregon, loaned us another two thousand dollars, we had just enough money to stay afloat while we awaited final word from S.S. White. That

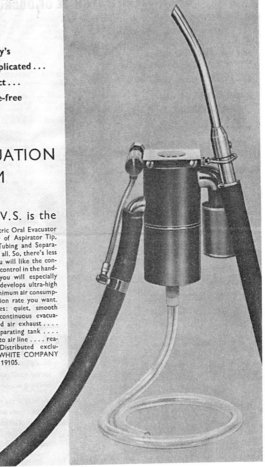

New!

**Here is today's
most uncomplicated . . .
most compact . . .
most trouble-free**

ORAL EVACUATION SYSTEM

A.V.S. is the

unique, non-electric Oral Evacuator consisting simply of Aspirator Tip, Venturi, Valve, Tubing and Separating Tank. That's all. So, there's less to go wrong. You will like the convenient fingertip control in the handpiece . . . . and you will especially like how A.V.S. develops ultra-high velocity with minimum air consumption for the suction rate you want. Other advantages: quiet, smooth operating . . . . continuous evacuation . . . . filtered air exhaust . . . . easy to clean separating tank . . . . readily attached to air line . . . . reasonable price. Distributed exclusively by S. S. WHITE COMPANY Philadelphia, Pa. 19105.

*Ken III and Loni called it the "super slobber sucker."
It was the invention that started it all.*

word came in February 1965 when S.S. White asked me to fly to corporate headquarters in Philadelphia. I told them that the company was short of money, and they agreed to pay for my flight and lodging. Arriving on February 19, I was presented with a ten-thousand-dollar check, a down payment on a twelve-thousand-dollar purchase order of two hundred units at sixty dollars apiece, which I promised to ship to them within ninety days. They also made clear that they had great faith in the product and expected that this would be just the first of many purchase orders. I called Joan with the good news, and we quickly agreed that Newberg, and not Colorado, should be the home of A-dec.

CHAPTER 8

BUTT TO BUTT IN THE HUT

With the ten-thousand-dollar check in my pocket, I returned to Newberg on Sunday, February 21, 1965, to begin the process of getting our new business up and running. I did so without Joan, as we had decided that I would temporarily live with my parents on the farm while she remained in Colorado, readying our home for sale and allowing the kids to finish the school year. We had several long talks before my departure as we made a list of all that needed to be accomplished in the coming weeks. We also set two goals for our new business—one general, and one more specific. The general goal was that A-dec didn't need to be big or make us a fortune. It just needed to make us proud. We wanted to provide the best products and the best service at a fair price. That simple goal is what we continue to strive for fifty years later. The specific goal was that A-dec would have ten employees in five years. Much to our surprise, we reached that goal within a matter of months.

My first order of business in Newberg was to locate a place to set up shop. The top candidate was a twenty-five-by-forty-foot Quonset hut in downtown Newberg. After a quick inspection, I concluded that this would fit our needs, and by five o'clock on Monday evening, I had rented the building for $110 a month. Over the next several days, I took care of a

Out of small acorns, mighty oaks grow. A-dec opened for business in this Quonset hut in February 1965.

laundry list of items—arranging for phones and electricity, ordering machinery and other materials, and buying insurance. Throughout these tasks, there were constant reminders of how much I needed Joan at my side. Not only did she know much more about insurance than I did, but many of the town's business leaders knew and respected Joan, and they were rightfully skeptical of my prospects for success, given my checkered employment history.

With the lights turned on at the Quonset hut, I went to work to fulfill the promise made to S.S. White that they would have their order of two hundred units by May 20. I contracted with a Portland manufacturing company to do the initial machining of the parts needed for the evacuators. They would then ship me the parts for the milling and drilling needed to finish them. This was accomplished on the manufacturing equipment that the check from S.S. White had allowed me to purchase—a milling machine, a lathe, a small bench grinder, and two drill presses. This equipment was all moved into the hut courtesy of a borrowed trailer and the help of Joan's brother and brother-in-law.

With Joan and the kids in Colorado, I was able to work around the clock those first months. Still, I never would have successfully met the S.S. White deadline without the help of Lucy Overton and Nan Hilger. Based on the recommendation of her son-in-law, who was a friend of mine, I hired Lucy as A-dec's first employee in March to help assemble evacuators. Two weeks later, I hired Nan, after her sister told me that she had lost her husband in a logging accident, and she needed a paycheck to support her two children. Nan's responsibilities were the same as Lucy's: assembly and light secondary work, which included drilling and soldering.

Lucy and Nan set the stage for what would soon become a tradition at A-dec: hiring women for manufacturing positions. Joan was the person most responsible for this hiring practice, as she was well aware that when we began and grew A-dec, Newberg had few decent-sized businesses except for a pulp mill. Women looking for employment were limited to seasonal jobs processing fruits and nuts. A-dec offered them year-round jobs in a clean and professional environment. I am also proud to note that Nan's daughter also worked at A-dec, and that her granddaughter and great-grandson are on our payroll, as well!

After the delivery of the first two hundred evacuators (meeting my ninety-day promise with one day to spare), we barely had time to catch our breath before S.S. White said they needed three hundred more. Additional orders soon came in from around the country as dentists who used the evacuators told other dentists of their effectiveness. I have never been so happy to see anyone as I was to see Joan, when she and the kids arrived home from Colorado in June 1965. We quickly agreed on a division of authority: I was in charge of making the products. Joan, who oversaw all personnel matters, as well as the financial and legal aspects of A-dec, was in charge of making the company. One of her first duties was payroll. If you promise not to tell the Internal Revenue Service, I will let you in on a little secret: for those first few months, I had simply given Lucy and Nan a hundred-dollar bill every time they completed eighty hours of work, assuring them that Joan would figure out the taxes when she got to Oregon.

However large her business responsibilities were, Joan never let them outweigh her responsibilities to our family. When the kids were growing up, Joan saw them off to school in the morning, and she was back home when the school day ended. And after Ken III and Loni went to bed, Joan was sometimes up most of the night doing payroll and paying the bills.

Entering the front door of the Quonset hut, Joan's desk, telephone, recipe box of possible customers, and filing cabinet were immediately to the left. My drafting board was on the right. A dividing wall with a door separated this tiny office from the machine shop in the back. With the addition of new employees, including Fred Plews, who would serve as my right hand man for many years, and Joan's sister, Lenora, who came aboard to help on the administrative side, space was so tight we began to joke that we were working "butt to butt in the hut."

Everyone pitched in to do what had to be done. A typical workday during our first year included going through the routines of any manufacturing company—bringing in supplies, cutting materials, drilling, soldering, assembling, testing, delivering finished pieces for nickel plating, and shipping. If the weather was sunny, we gained extra elbow room by packaging evacuators on the sidewalk in front of the hut. At the end of the day, we loaded the evacuators and tips in our station wagon and drove them to the loading dock of a local freight service. When we became such regular customers that the freight service began coming to our office to pick up packages, we felt we had really made it.

Those first months were immensely satisfying ones as orders began to pour in. We were forced to rent a building adjacent to the Quonset hut to give our rapidly expanding workforce the room they needed. The July 28, 1965, edition of our hometown community newspaper, *The Newberg Graphic,* reported on our success under the headline "Bright Future Seen For New Dental Firm," and before long, it seemed as if the whole town was talking about A-dec.

CHAPTER 9

INNOVATION AND EXPANSION

I t's not every company that is indebted to a nineteenth-century English dentist, but that is the case with A-dec. Historians of the dental practice say that it was a London dentist named Alfred Coleman who, in 1882, first suggested the concept of dentists sitting rather than the long-held practice of standing while they examined patients. It was not until the mid-twentieth century, however, that the practice of sit-down dentistry took hold and dentists discovered that the equipment they had been using while standing was not suited to the sit-down concept.

Other changes and innovations in the dental field were occurring at the same time as this transition. Thanks to faster and more powerful drills and advancements like the A-dec oral evacuation device, large, bulky dental units with electric motors were no longer required, and dentists were less encumbered. With a dental assistant on one side using suction and syringe, and the dentist on the other with a drill in one hand and a mirror in the other, the term *four-handed dentistry* became popular, and several generations of equipment became obsolete almost overnight. In short, there was a vacuum, and A-dec was ready to fill that vacuum with a series of new products that, along with the continued success of the oral evacuator, would spur the company to grow beyond Joan's and my wildest dreams.

My greatest frustration during my checkered job history was that my passion for solving problems and trying to make something better, simpler, smaller, or less expensive usually led to my getting fired. Now that Joan and I were in charge, that frustration was no longer an issue. With Joan running the day-to-day operations, I was free to dream, design, and draw as chief "imagineer," and dentists were inspiring my imagination.

It began in the summer of 1965 when Portland dentist Dr. Ken Jensen asked me to develop a mounting device flexible enough to put his A-dec oral evacuator and other instruments right at his fingertips. The solution was the Dec-Et, a small four-by-four-inch square steel post that bolted to the floor and included built-in air and water filters, air and water shut-off valves, two electrical outlets, and an instrument holder, where you could mount the air-vacuum system and the control for the dental drill.

That same summer, Idaho dentist Dr. Sam Winn shared with me an idea he had after his wife told him of a movable cart her beautician used to keep her scissors, brushes, and other tools within easy reach. Dr. Winn thought the same concept might work in his office, and he built a similar cart where his dental assistant could place the tools of the dental trade. Dr. Winn believed his tray cart might have some sales potential in the industry, but he had no experience or interest in manufacturing and selling a product. He was impressed with A-dec's reputation, and he offered us the opportunity to take his product to market. Joan and I tinkered with his design, making a number of improvements, and soon A-dec was offering the Formica-covered Tray-Cart, which provided a

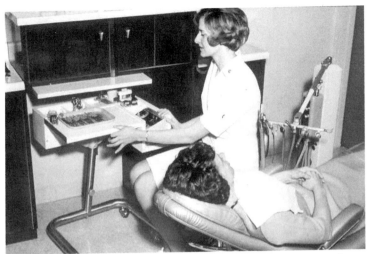

The Tray-Cart and Dec-et allowed the dental team to work seated instead of standing.

seated dental assistant with a stable work surface for instruments and supplies. We soon had seven models from which to choose.

We knew we had a product that was twice as functional and lower in cost than what was currently being used in dental offices, and we set out on the dental trade-show circuit to make some sales. We immediately ran into trouble at a major trade show in New York City. When our shipping crates with the Tray-Cart display arrived at the hotel exhibition space, we were told in blunt terms by union representatives that we couldn't unpack the boxes by ourselves and that we had to hire a union carpenter to do that work. I explained that I had built the packing crates myself and would open them myself. He then made it clear that if we wanted to have a booth at the show, then at the very least we needed to hire a carpenter to watch me open the box. It cost us fifty dollars to follow his advice, and it taught me my first lesson on working with labor unions.

As Joan and I set up our display, we couldn't help but notice that as a new and unknown business, our booth was located in the least-desirable place possible—near the entrance to a stairwell accessed by a door. And when the door was open, our booth was cut in half. We also noticed to our chagrin that all our clothes gave off the slight odor of printer's ink. We had received our rush order of product literature right before we left Oregon for New York and had packed it in our suitcase while it must still have been drying. The smell lingered all the way through the show. A final thumb in our eye came when three executives from one of the industry's top companies stopped by our display of Tray-Carts and one remarked, "They're cute, but they'll never sell." Joan and I winced when we heard that remark, but we were confident that dentists were in the market for equipment that was more compact, more accessible, and more convenient than anything previously available. The Tray-Carts we took to New York were in step with the times, regardless of snide remarks from our competitors. Fifty years after we introduced it, the Tray-Cart continues as one of our best-selling products.

Another item was added to our inventory when Roseburg, Oregon, dentist Dr. Leland Van Allen called A-dec in June 1965 and explained that his office had been destroyed by an exploding water heater, and he asked if we offered a portable dental unit that he could use in a temporary location until his office was restored. My first answer was no, but that was quickly replaced by my second answer—not yet. I immediately went to work, building a portable Denta-Cart that would allow dentists to sit down and be able to work on their patients without reaching or stretching for anything they needed. Driving Denta-Cart sales was the fact that we built them one at a time,

designed with K.I.S.S.* in mind

tray cart

The first **MOBILE** operatory cart that allows the dentist and assistant to remain seated during entire operation. Variable height with positive lock . . . Over 25 possible compartment arrangements. **$250**

dec et

The compact stand designed so that optional components such as handpieces and control box, syringe, oral evacuator, and saliva ejector, may be easily attached. **$295**

denta cart

The complete air-operated **MOBILE** Dental Unit. Standard equipment includes instrument holders, saliva ejector, oral evacuator, water tank, waste collection jar and quick disconnects. **$550**

＊Keep It Simple and Serviceable

We believe in the idea of Simplicity in design, operation and maintenance by using standard components of the highest quality.

SEE OUR BOOTH IN NEW YORK, CHICAGO AND SAN FRANCISCO

P.O. Box 111 • Newberg, Oregon 97132
Phone 503 / 538-2303

A-dec's first advertisement promoted three products that helped spur the company's growth.

encouraging individual dentists to specify exactly how they wanted their carts built.

An important landmark in the history of A-dec occurred in the late fall of 1968, when representatives of Den-Tal-Ez, one of the giants of the industry, approached Joan and me at the American Dental Association's trade show in Miami with a proposition. Could A-dec design and manufacture carts and dental units that Den-Tal-Ez would then sell as companions to their dental chairs? An agreement was quickly reached, and thanks to Den-Tal-Ez's excellent sales force, our cart sales quadrupled in the first year of the partnership and tripled in the second. To keep up with the demand, we increased our workforce by 400 percent in just one year.

Another key factor in our early success was the partnership we were able to form with dental schools across the country. John Hilterbrant, one of our first independent sales representatives, was based in Chicago and introduced our products to dental schools in the Midwest. By March 1967, A-dec products could be found in dental schools at the University of Iowa, Northwestern University, and Loyola University of Chicago. Marquette, Temple, and the University of Missouri soon followed.

Today, A-dec holds contracts with sixty-five of the sixty-eight accredited dental schools in the United States. This overwhelming vote of support is due in part to the quality of our products and in part to our spirit of adventure and our willingness to experiment in unorthodox ways. It was and is typical of dental schools to ask "Can you do this?" More often than not, what they needed was something that was not being done. This meant we were tackling things we had never heard of, which put us ahead of our competition. For example, in

1967 we produced a student unit for Marquette University that included a hand-piece control, a syringe, and two dental drills. Everything was self-contained within a convenient carrying case, giving the student the ability to carry the unit from the teaching lab to the clinic to his or her locker.

We also found a good customer in Uncle Sam, as in 1969, when we developed a Porta-Cart for the United States military. It was a self-contained unit that could be used in the field, requiring only a compressed air source to operate.

Things were going so well those first years that it seemed even our mistakes turned out to work in our favor. In 1969, I traveled to Washington, DC, to make a presentation to a group of military dentists in hopes of receiving a government contract for a version of the Porta-Cart that I had developed especially for use in the field. Unfortunately, I had neglected to test the unit I had brought along. As I began my demonstration, I immediately realized that the unit's air and water lines were reversed. As a result, the water bottle began bubbling like someone blowing air through a straw into a glass of water. When I tried to correct the problem by disconnecting the air supply, the air line filled up with water, which oozed all over the carpet. I stopped the air flow, turned the unit upside down, and emptied the water into a waste paper basket. Using a pocketknife and pair of pliers to reverse the connections, I profusely apologized, then proceeded with the demonstration. All the while, I could hear the group whispering. It was easy to imagine they were all agreeing that this rube from Oregon was a waste of their time.

I left the room convinced my opportunity had flown out the window and told the folks from Den-Tal-Ez, who were supposed to work out the details of the government contract, that I had flopped. All of a sudden, one of the Den-Tal-Ez salesmen came into the room with a big smile on his face and said, "Ken, you slayed them! They have a few minor changes, but said that anything that can be fixed with a pocket knife and a pair of pliers is just what they need out in the field!"

Our "marriage" with Den-Tal-Ez was instrumental in A-dec's growth, and, ironically, so, too, was our "divorce" from Den-Tal Ez. Our agreement was that Den-Tal-Ez would purchase the carts and the chair-mounted units (which we had added to our manufacturing repertoire) at one-third the retail price they charged their customers. In the fall of 1972, Joan and I noticed that they raised their retail price by 15 percent, but only gave us a 2.5 percent increase. When we asked them to explain, they told us it was none of our business. Joan and I were very uncomfortable in doing business with a company that so clearly violated an agreement, so we told Den-Tal-Ez executives that it was time to pull the plug. We negotiated a two-year separation agreement, which would give them time to get geared up to make their own products and give us time to establish and grow our own sales force.

Conventional wisdom in the industry was that since Den-Tal-Ez manufactured chairs and we didn't, they would retain 70 percent of the cart and chair-mounted-unit business we had developed together, as most dentists preferred buying all their equipment from one manufacturer. That ratio was something I couldn't accept, and Joan and I quickly made the decision that A-dec needed to manufacture our own dental chairs. That is just what we did, and the result was a total reversal of what was predicted: we kept 70 percent of the business, and Den-Tal-Ez got 30 percent.

As our business in the United States continued to skyrocket, a logical next step was to expand to the international market. In 1973, I traveled to Europe on a fact-finding mission to study dental practices and to determine if there was room in the market for A-dec. I returned to Newberg with more questions than answers. Dentists in each country seemed to have differences in the size and style of equipment they preferred. What worked in Sweden might not work in Italy. Would it be worth it to manufacture a different product for each country? Any company that was successful in the overseas market also had a warehouse where they could ship and store products. Who would operate an A-dec warehouse, and how could we know from thousands of miles away that it was being operated with efficiency? Would it be too difficult and cumbersome to navigate import rules and regulations in each country? All of these questions led me to conclude that entering the international market was just too complicated. By 1975, however, it became clear that the possible increase in sales made it worth finding satisfactory answers to those questions. After additional study, Joan and I hired Joe Plews as our first international sales manager, and we have never looked back. Today, A-dec products can be found in 130 countries, A-dec warehouses are located in England and Australia, and international sales account for 20 percent of our business.

As the years went by, each new product we manufactured seemed to lead to another new product, and by 1982, A-dec had the capability to provide dentists with all the fundamental components needed to set up a clinic or office practice. Fast-forwarding to the present, A-dec, which began in Newberg in February 1965 with a handful of employees in a twenty-four-by-forty Quonset hut, now occupies thirteen buildings on a fifty-acre campus that contains over 650,000 square feet of manufacturing and administrative space and a workforce of over one thousand. Joan and I were asked many times to explain the success of our company, and our answer was always the same. A-dec's success is rooted in fifteen principles that comprise what has come to be known as "The A-dec Way."

CHAPTER 10

THE A-DEC WAY

For the first decade of A-dec's history, Joan and I were able to devote most of our attention to the priorities of product development and building successful customer relationships, while also handling the countless details that are part and parcel of running a small business. But as our sales and our payroll continued to expand, we came to the realization that A-dec was no longer a mom-and-pop operation, and in April 1975 we hired a general manager who we hoped would remove some of the work from our plate and who could assist us in developing a strategic plan for the future. This decision led to the creation of a document that is to A-dec what the Constitution is to the United States in that it has governed our day-to-day operations for nearly forty years.

Joan and I couldn't help but laugh over the years about the fact that a document that has been so influential to the success of A-dec and that has been taught by universities in their business colleges and MBA programs was the result of a disagreement over something as seemingly insignificant as the color of ink!

It all began when the new general manager we hired ordered new invoices from a printing company that offered a cheaper price than the one we had been using. The problem was that

Joan and I had worked years before with an artist to develop our company logo, and the logo had always been printed in a certain shade of green we called "A-dec green." When I saw the new invoices, the first detail I noticed was that the logo was not quite the same green it used to be. I asked our general manager to explain, and he reported that it was a cost-saving measure, and the precise color of ink didn't make a real difference. Now, in the grand scheme of things, I know his decision probably made sense. At the time, however, I was furious, explaining to him that "No detail, however small, should be ignored, and while big business might not care about the consistency of the color of the logo, A-dec does."

In hopes of understanding each other and avoiding future disagreements, Joan and I took the advice of a respected business consultant and invited the general manager and a small team of trusted employees to join with us in identifying the core values of A-dec. The group met on three occasions in the conference room of a local hotel, and as the conversation went on and ideas flew back and forth, Joan took the lead in refining our words and ideas into a final document. That document, titled "The A-dec Way," lists fifteen principles that are at the heart of the way we do business and the way we treat our employees. The document has not been changed or modified since it was written, and I hope it never will be. Of all the awards and honors that came to A-dec over the years, the ones in which we took the most pride was our annual listing by the *Portland Business Journal* as one of the "Best Places to Work" and as one of Oregon's "Most Admired" companies. Those awards speak to the effectiveness and value of the following fifteen principles.

1. Concern for people

One of the benefits of having so many jobs before Joan and I started A-dec was the fact that I experienced quite a few work environments and factory floors. I made a pledge to myself early on that if I ever ran a business, it would be a pleasant place where people wanted to work and enjoyed working. Thanks in large part to Joan's touch, that is exactly what we have at A-dec. From the very beginning, A-dec has been infused with a real feeling of family. We treat our employees like a family because that's the only way I know how to run a business.

Joan and I built the company on the concept of having the best people possible, treating them as we would like to be treated, and considering them and their needs and wants in all our decisions. Under Joan's leadership, A-dec buildings and factory floors are immaculate. Walls are painted in comfortable colors, and music is piped in to every department. Free tea and coffee are available to employees at all times. We have a spacious employee cafeteria and dining room, and we have an outside Japanese garden for good weather brown bagging. Joan also refurbished her parents' house and turned it into a company meeting facility, where she vacuumed, set out fresh cut flowers, and baked cookies. In addition, A-dec employees are the beneficiaries of a profit-sharing program, and, of course, have a top-rate health care plan.

The concern that Joan and I show for our employees has been returned to us more times and in more ways than we could ever have imagined, including with a Christmas present that meant more to Joan and me than all the civic and business honors we have been privileged to receive. Imagine our surprise when, in 1978, A-dec employees pooled their donations and purchased the very Quonset hut that was the first home of our company. They found the hut being used by a local farmer to house sheep and pigs. They not only bought and cleaned the hut, but they also installed a new building in its place for the farmer.

Along with concern for our employees, concern for our customers is also in the DNA of A-dec. We maintain no sales quotas, ensuring that our salespeople concentrate on building strong relationships with customers rather than simply increasing sales. Joan and I believed that one of the best ways to show concern for our customers is to actually listen to them. We check each day to see if any of our doctors or dealers are having trouble with our products. If something is reported, we deal with the problem so it doesn't happen again. I remember one time when Kenny and I were at an industry conference, and we were visiting with a gentleman who marketed A-dec products in the southeastern United States. "You know that the problem with you guys is that you don't open until eleven o'clock Eastern time," he said. "There are times when I have been out on a service call first thing in the morning, and needed some help in answering a question, but have to sit around and wait until you open." Kenny and I nodded our heads, and the moment we got back to Newberg, we changed procedures so a customer service representative would start each morning at five o'clock Oregon time, which was eight o'clock Eastern time.

2. *Provide for opportunity and assist in self-development*

A-dec provides opportunities for employees to move up the leadership ladder. We promote from within, and Joan created a tuition-reimbursement program for those wanting to further their educations. In fact, the first individual who volunteered to work the five o'clock customer service shift spent his afternoons earning a master's degree, completely paid for by A-dec.

3. Provide an atmosphere encouraging self-satisfaction and pride

During my years as an employee, nothing bothered me more than a supervisor hovering over my shoulder, assuming that I would make a mistake at any moment. The atmosphere is radically different at A-dec. Joan and I believe that if each employee takes responsibility for the quality of his or her own work, then there was no need for quality control inspectors. Employees who make the parts and assemble them into the finished products perform their own quality control work. Individual employee quality control is better than having a bunch of tin-god inspectors running around the place. It encourages people to take pride in what they do.

4. Encourage team effort

Another lesson I learned during my checkered work history was that directives and orders sent down from the executive suite without any discussion or input from the rank-and-file employees were directives that could used a healthy dose of improvement and common sense. A-dec employees are urged to meet regularly in groups of twenty to talk about all parts of our operation and to make suggestions for improvements. There are no "silos" at A-dec, with people hoarding information. We are all part of the same team.

5. Maintain complete fairness, honesty, and integrity

Call us old-fashioned, but Joan and I believed there was no such thing as "almost" fair or "almost" honest. We told the truth, the whole truth, and nothing but the truth to our employees, vendors, and customers—and we expected the same in return.

What most companies call sick leave, we call paid time off, as this reflects our belief that honesty is the best policy. We didn't want our employees calling in sick on a given day if what they really planned was a three-day weekend or a trip up the river to catch a fish. We didn't want them to think they had to lie about it in order to get a day off.

Joan and I were so committed to honesty that we were willing to give up seventeen million dollars when a customer wasn't being fair and honest with us. As sales of our products continued to increase, Joan and I made the decision that we would no longer build private-label dental units. We wanted everything we produced to have the A-dec name on it. When HealthCo, the second-largest distributor of our products, asked us to build a private-label dental unit for them, we turned them down. HealthCo continued to buy from A-dec, but they also worked with another company to produce their own dental unit. When that product hit the market, they became a competitor of ours. Word also reached me that some HealthCo managers were falsely telling prospective customers that their products were, in fact, built by A-dec.

Joan and I agreed that their dishonest behavior meant that we could no longer do business with them. At the time, their seventeen-million-dollar account was 18 percent of our business. If we had looked the other way, however, and rewarded their behavior, then Joan and I wouldn't have been able to look at ourselves in the mirror. We pulled the plug on their account, and our other customers soon made up that 18 percent and more.

6. Maintain open, consistent, and regular communication

When we were working "butt to butt in the hut" it was easy for employees to talk with us, and as the company payroll doubled and redoubled many times, we maintained the same atmosphere. We were "Ken" and "Joan" not "Mr. and Mrs. Austin," and every employee knew they had carte blanche to come to us with a suggestion or a problem.

7. Encourage public service

Joan and I created quite a buzz in Newberg in A-dec's first year when members of the local volunteer Fire Department came to the A-dec hut to sell tickets for the annual community Thanksgiving "Turkey Carnival." They were expecting us to buy one ticket. Instead, we bought ten—one for each of our employees. We continued the tradition of buying a ticket for each A-dec employee for fifty years—even when we had a thousand employees. Giving back to our community and helping those in need is a value that was instilled in Joan and me by our parents, and it's one that we put at the very heart of A-dec.

Perhaps Joan put it best when she said, "Ken and I give because we feel a responsibility to give back. We have been very fortunate in our life's occupation. It only seems appropriate to share our bountiful harvest. It feels so good to give when you know it will make someone's life a little easier or happier. We're grateful for the joys of making others happy. The rewards are great!"

With so many worthy causes to choose from, Joan and I focused our philanthropic efforts on three priorities. First, since the community of Newberg had been so supportive to A-dec and to us, and since the majority of our employees lived in Newberg, we looked for ways to give back to the community. We wanted Newberg to be a healthy community, so Joan led the effort to raise money for a new community hospital in Newberg. When the Portland-based Oregon Symphony asked us for our support, we responded that we would be happy to make a contribution—with the stipulation that the symphony would perform an annual free concert in Newberg, thereby saving our employees and their families the time and expense of driving to Portland. And when Special Olympics Oregon came to us with a plan that would bring their annual statewide summer games to Newberg, filling our local motels and restaurants with athletes and coaches, we quickly offered our support, and delighted in experiencing the smiles of more than a thousand Special Olympics athletes marching onto the Newberg High School football field.

Our second philanthropic priority was Oregon State University. OSU played such a major role in my life by allowing me to follow my passions, and Joan and I both believed that we needed to "pay it forward" by helping young people follow theirs.

Of the gifts we have made to OSU, the one that probably meant the most to us was the gift that created the Austin Family Business Program. This program was Joan's idea and arose from our desire to help family businesses like ours avoid problems and pitfalls that result in the fact that only about 30 percent of family-owned businesses survive into the second generation, 12 percent are still viable in the third generation, and only 3 percent operate into the fourth generation and beyond.

The innovative program offers a series of classes and seminars that prepare family businesses to balance the well-being of the business and the family as they address the unique challenges and opportunities that arise day to day and most especially during succession. It was incredibly gratifying to have people tell us that their participation in the program gave them the knowledge to save a family business.

I also take special pride in the Austin Entrepreneur Program, which is jointly administered by OSU's colleges of business and engineering. The AEP is designed to assist students who think differently, work differently, and think outside the box. Remind you of anyone?

How I wish Joan could have been with me at the OSU campus on October 31, 2014, for the grand opening of Austin Hall. This hundred-thousand-square-foot building will serve as the home of the OSU College of Business.

Austin Hall, home of OSU's College of Business, was dedicated in 2014.

Photo by Karl Maasdam

With Benny Beaver at the October 31, 2014, dedication of Austin Hall.

Our third charitable priority centers around causes of special interest to the dental industry, including offering A-dec equipment to dental schools and students across the country at minimal or no cost. Joan and I took great pride in the fact that nearly every dental school in the United States features A-dec equipment.

One of the true joys in my life has been my membership in the Newberg Rotary and our involvement in a program called Rota-Dent, which is a partnership between A-dec, W&H Dentalwerk of Austria, and Rotary International. Rota-Dent had its providential beginning in 1965 when I made a sales call in Portland. Upon moving to Newberg earlier that year, I had joined one of the community's two Rotary International clubs and frequently wore my Rotary lapel pin. The manager I was calling upon noticed my pin and casually mentioned, "I see that you're a member of Kiwanis." I corrected him by letting him know that I was a Rotarian. "No matter," he responded. "I have an idea that might interest you."

He then told me the story of a dentist he knew who was ready to retire and was willing to donate his equipment to dentists who accept missionary assignments in third-world countries. He asked if A-dec could help get the equipment into the right hands. I was intrigued by the story and his question, and at the next meeting of my Rotary club, I made a point of seeking out Dr. John Gearin, a dentist and long-time friend. I told him what I had heard, and his first response was to ask, "Who will provide repairs and maintenance to the equipment used in the field?" He had a point. The equipment the dentist wanted to donate was old and vulnerable. The last thing I wanted to do was provide equipment to a volunteer dentist and have the equipment not work or quickly break.

John then said, "Maybe you have something you can substitute that's newer." Until then, I had not thought about giving dental equipment away, but the more I thought about it, the more I liked it. We soon began to donate equipment that came from returns, demonstrations, and repaired items that could not be resold. The donations were quickly snapped up by a variety of missionary programs, and in 1967 I designed a special portable field unit that included an oral evacuator, an air/water syringe, a foot control, a self-contained water system, high- and low-speed hand pieces, a tripod stand, and a maintenance kit.

For an assembly and packaging crew, I initially recruited Boy Scouts from Newberg's Explorer Post and put them to work in a barn near our family farmhouse. Soon, the jobs became a project for Newberg Rotarians and A-dec employees who were willing to give up an occasional Saturday. Eventually, the tasks were moved back inside A-dec, so the units could progress through our rigorous quality control system quicker and at less cost.

I am proud to report that the Rota-Dent program and distribution of Rota-Dent units continues today and is overseen by a board of five directors, consisting of two members from each of the two Newberg Rotary Clubs and one Austin family representative, as well as a nonvoting A-Dec liaison.

Joan also shared my pride in the fact that our children and grandchildren share our passion for giving back to our community. Ken III has devoted his time and talents to many causes, including Rotary and the Boy Scouts of America. Loni was the driving force behind the revitalization of Newberg's downtown, where her gallery, Art Elements, is always abuzz with activity. She also helped plan and design the Chehalem

Cultural Arts Center in Newberg, which has added a great deal to Yamhill County. Both Ken III and Loni surprised Joan and me on Christmas Day 2004 when they told us they had created a philanthropic fund for our grandchildren. Since then, the five grandchildren have joined in reviewing projects submitted to us by the Oregon Community Foundation and selecting those that we would support.

8. Encourage creativity

I often describe myself not as an engineer but as an "imagineer." The message Joan and I sent out and that was infused at every level of A-dec is that all ideas and suggestions are welcome, and that innovation and new ideas are what started A-dec and what continue to drive our success.

9. Commitment to productivity and quality

I recall the time when we discovered a minor cosmetic defect on one of the chairs we were manufacturing. The defect was so small that it would have been undetected by our customers. Yet, without hesitation, we opened and inspected more than three hundred shipping cases to see if the defect had been repeated on another chair. The defect had not been repeated, and not one employee complained about the time spent opening the cases and inspecting the chairs. Quality control at A-dec is never second-guessed and is everyone's responsibility.

We recognize that productivity with quality is the only real security for a company and its people in the American enterprise system. We commit to seeking better methods and equipment—there is always a better way.

10. Maintain consistency

By urging consistency, Joan and I weren't urging A-dec employees to do the same thing the same way all the time. Rather, we were highlighting the value in using a steady and predictable approach when conducting business. Our vendors and our customers could always rely on the fact that when they dealt with A-dec, they knew they would be treated consistently with honesty, courtesy, and respect.

11. Dedication to improvement

Suggesting improvements to a procedure or a product led to my getting fired on several occasions. The truth is, I probably could have been a little more diplomatic in expressing my opinions, but any business that is not receptive to ideas and efforts for improvement is a business that will ultimately fail. Joan and I encouraged and welcomed all suggestions, and everyone at A-dec is empowered to find what's wrong and fix it.

12. Keep things simple and basic

Joan and I learned growing up on a farm that if a piece of machinery breaks, it needs to be fixed quickly and easily so crops are not lost. The same is true in a dentist's office. All A-dec equipment is designed with simplicity in mind, because it should be as easy to maintain a dental unit as it is to change a light bulb. The A-dec philosophy is that any product we sell to a dentist can be maintained by a dentist.

13. Build on a basis of "need"

Over the years, I have seen many companies that add something dentists don't need to one of their products just because the new feature might pump up the marketing pizzazz. A-dec has succeeded because rather than building on the basis of emotion, we build on the basis of need. As I've written, many of our most successful products were the result of dentists telling us what they needed to better perform their jobs. Joan and I were also constantly putting ourselves in other people's shoes and asking whether or not our products were filling a dentist's need. If they weren't filling a need, then we weren't doing our jobs.

14. Attention to detail

It was attention to detail—the shade of green ink in our logo—that led to the creation of "The A-dec Way." Joan and I agreed that if you didn't pay attention to the small things, then you soon wouldn't be paying attention to the big things.

15. Conserve resources

Growing up in the Depression, Joan and I learned early in life that every dollar counted and that nothing—be it food, nails, clothes or time—should be wasted. In the manufacturing process, A-dec uses the least amount of material possible in the making of a part. Simply put, using four machines to make a part is better than using six machines.

THE SIX-WAY TEST

Along with fifteen principles, the A-dec Way also includes a challenge to our employees to ask themselves six questions as they go about their work. This Six-Way Test was adapted from the famous Four-Way Test that is familiar to all Rotarians, and which Joan and I found very inspirational. The Four-Way Test is an ethical guide for Rotarians to use for their personal and professional relationships. The Four-Way Test is:

> *Of the things we think, say, or do,*
> - *Is it the TRUTH?*
> - *Is it FAIR to all concerned?*
> - *Will it build GOODWILL and BETTER FRIENDSHIPS?*
> - *Will it be BENEFICIAL to all concerned?*

The A-dec Six-Way Test is as follows:
1. Is there a need?
2. Is this the simplest and best way to do it?
3. Am I using time and material effectively?
4. Am I helping make A-dec better for everyone?
5. Can I be proud of what we are doing?
6. Have I communicated?

If the answer to all those questions is yes, then there is no doubt that the decision made or the action taken is the correct one.

CHAPTER 11

MY SPIRITUAL JOURNEY

A business that was succeeding beyond my wildest dreams. A wonderful, fulfilling marriage. Two great children. Anyone looking at my life in the 1970s might have concluded that I had it all. They would have been wrong. Yes, I had all those attributes of a successful life. But I also had a problem. I was drinking heavily, and I was addicted to alcohol. In short, I was an alcoholic.

I had my first drink and got drunk for the first time when I was fourteen years old and celebrating on New Year's Eve. I didn't drink again until the next New Year's Eve. In high school, however, my once-a-year binges expanded to include an occasional party or beer bust. College social life provided even more opportunities for drinking. Every Friday there was a party, and I didn't miss out. During my years in the military, I made off-duty visits to the bar in the officer's club where I was stationed. I was able to rationalize my drinking throughout these times as it never got me into trouble. I didn't drink and drive. There were no brushes with the law. My marriage was strong. I was hard working and hard charging. Life was good, and life would be better after another drink.

My attitude began to change in the 1970s. While no one knew I had a problem as I never drank during the day, I became more aware that alcohol had become my social lubricant in the evenings. I relied on it to feel more relaxed around other people. It allowed me to dance more, mingle more, and talk more. I would also drink when I arrived home from the office, telling myself I was dehydrated from working too hard. I might start with a cold beer, then progress to a gin and tonic, and I would wake up in the middle of the night still on the couch where I passed out watching television. I would have the shakes so bad in the morning that I couldn't hold anything with a fork. The only way I could eat breakfast was to make a scrambled egg sandwich, holding the toast with both hands.

In February 1981, I neared a breaking point and reached out for help. I had long admired Hal Pearson, president of Den-Tal-Ez. Hal was a successful executive who had risen to the top of his company, and he was very public with the fact that his success came only after he found sobriety. At a dental industry conference in Chicago, I asked Hal if he would make time for a private meeting. He took one look at me and said, "You have a problem." During the conversation that followed, Hal credited Alcoholics Anonymous as the driving force behind his sobriety, and he urged me to attend a meeting. He also went to his briefcase, pulled out a book titled *Search for Serenity* by Lewis Presnall, and explained how it helped to change his life and how he thought it could help change mine as well.

I thought a great deal about Hal's advice over the next several days. When I returned to Oregon, however, I convinced myself that Hal's problem was worse than mine, and I didn't need to attend AA meetings. I did take his other suggestion and ordered a copy of *Search for Serenity* from the Utah Alcohol Foundation. The book arrived a few weeks later, and I was immediately impressed with Presnall's writing and his analysis of the mental problems that accompany addiction. Included in the same package as the book was a list of other publications from the Utah Alcohol Foundation, which included another book written by Presnall, *Alcohol and the Exposed Family*. As the weeks and months went by, I would turn again and again to the book, reading a few pages at a time.

My life was transformed on the morning of January 1, 1982. The family and I were at our beach house on the Oregon coast. I was up before anyone else and opened Presnall's book again as I sat in our living room. I read the book from cover to cover. I was suddenly struck by the realization that all I had to do was admit I was powerless over alcohol. Just then, I looked outside the window and saw a seagull flying by. It dawned on me that a power greater than myself created that seagull, and the same power created what I could see outside that window—the grass, the wind, the waves, the sand. I began weeping, knowing that it was time to turn my life over to a power greater than self.

When Joan and Loni came out of their bedrooms I said for the first time that I was an alcoholic and that I couldn't drink anymore. Loni said, "Oh, Dad, you're not alcoholic, you just drank too much last night." I repeated again in no uncertain terms that I was an alcoholic. Now that I had admitted to myself and to my family that I was an alcoholic, there were others I wanted to tell and begin making amends. The first person I called when we returned from the beach on January 4 was our minister in Newberg. He came right over, listened to my story, prayed with me, and said that there was somebody in Newberg he wanted me to meet. Several hours later, I received a phone call from a physician named Greg Skipper. I knew Dr. Skipper as a friend of Ken III, but I didn't know why he was calling. He said that my minister had asked him to call because he had the same problem that I had, and he invited me to join him at an Alcoholics Anonymous meeting in Portland the very next evening. I accepted the invitation, but my first AA meeting was not a good experience. The problem was not the counselor or the other participants. The problem was me. As I listened to the other attendees share the story of the choices that led them to an AA meeting, I concluded that I was different than them. I never drank on the job. I never got divorced. I never was arrested for drinking and driving. My dismissive attitude did not go unnoticed. When the meeting was over, an attendee walked up to me and said, "You won't get sober if you don't change." What I would later learn is that many first-time AA participants reacted as I did—by convincing themselves that his or her problem was unique.

Still looking for a venue where I would be comfortable in discussing my problem, I telephoned the Oregon Council on Alcohol and Drug Addiction, described the kind of meeting I was searching for, and asked for a recommendation. They told me of a group in a nearby community that consisted of lawyers, executives, and other business professionals. I attended this group for a few sessions, but still didn't feel entirely comfortable. I then learned of an AA group in Portland that was limited to doctors, dentists, and veterinarians. I contacted the doctor who led the group, who said that he had heard of A-dec and gave me permission to attend, even though I wasn't technically eligible to do so. I was warmly greeted at the meeting and felt very comfortable with the other members. At the second meeting, however, I detected a certain coolness. By the third meeting, one of the other members asked out loud, "Why is Ken here, when I can't bring my neighbor who is an attorney."

Realizing I was out of place, I immediately walked out. The doctor who had invited me followed me and begged me not to go out and drink. It was like he had read my mind. Unable to find a support system necessary to back up my resolve to stay sober, I was ready to give up. Thankfully, he understood this, convinced me not to give up, and urged me to see an individual named Dr. Kent Neff. The former head of the psychiatric unit at Portland's Providence Hospital, Dr. Neff specialized in working with doctors and dentists reported to the state medical board for alcohol or drug abuse.

I had reached ninety days of sobriety when I first sat in front of Dr. Neff and started to talk. A year of one-on-one meetings later, I was still talking and he was still listening and counseling. I had not had a drink for over a year, but I was still searching for a better understanding of myself and my disease. It was then that he recommended I attend a treatment center. My vision of a treatment center was a program near Portland where I would attend sessions in the morning and return to Newberg in the afternoon to check in at the office before going home. Dr. Neff quickly set me straight, announcing that he was sending me to a California-based treatment program at Children's Hospital of Orange County (CHOC), which had a record of successfully changing lives.

With the full of support of Joan and the family, I flew to California for what was to be the most transformational two weeks of my life. It is difficult to put into words exactly what occurred during those two weeks. Perhaps the best way to explain it is that through conversations, counseling, and reflection, I understood myself and my addiction better than I ever had before, and I learned how to handle day-to-day problems without the crutch of alcohol.

The Hazelden Springbrook treatment facility, which has changed countless lives for the better.

In the years that followed, I would remain in touch with Dr. Neff and my counselors from CHOC. Dr. Neff and I were talking on the phone one day in 1987 when he expressed an interest in building an alcohol treatment center in Oregon, so that those battling addiction issues would not have to travel out of state. Knowing the change that a center had made in my life, Joan and I were intrigued by the idea and invited Dr. Neff to Newberg for further discussions. There, he further detailed his proposal to build a center near Portland. He was frank in admitting that the parcel of land he had identified as an ideal location was terribly expensive, and that he didn't have the money to close the deal. Joan and I had previously purchased a parcel of land close to A-dec headquarters in anticipation of expansion of our manufacturing facility. We had subsequently determined it really wasn't suited for that purpose, and we

raised the idea with Dr. Neff of building his facility in Newberg. He declined, expressing his desire that his center would be targeted to business professionals, and he thought it was important to be easily accessible to the Portland airport.

A month later, Dr. Neff called to ask if our property was still available. It was, and Joan and I, joined by the remarkable Sonja Haugen, a longtime key employee of Austin Industries, began working on the design of what we would name the Springbrook Institute. Joan and I agreed that key to the design was a family-friendly environment, as I had noticed during my stay at CHOC that there were no areas that provided privacy for visiting families, and that our meals were hospital food served on a hospital tray. June 1988 marked the beginning of construction on the twenty-three-acre campus, which included a fifty-two-bed residential building, a clinic, and an administration building. When the facility was fully operational that fall, Joan and I felt a great deal of satisfaction with the knowledge that we were part of something that would change lives for the better.

Joan and I received one-third of the Springbrook stock in exchange for the land we provided, but we continued to devote all our attention to A-dec and did not pay as much attention as we should have to the financial bottom line of Springbrook. The scope of the financial difficulties led to the 1991 departure of Dr. Neff and to Springbrook being placed into receivership. Loni bluntly told her mother and me that it was our responsibility to keep the doors open so more people could be helped and that we should buy Springbrook back from the bank. We followed her advice, and thanks to Sonja, who became chief executive officer, and Joan, who served as chairman of the board, Springbrook became financially stable and earned a reputation as one of the most respected and successful addiction treatment facilities in the Pacific Northwest. The many individuals who have come up to Joan or me to thank us for helping save a loved one's life are special— even spiritual—experiences and have made our investment worth every penny.

On December 31, 2001, we sold Springbrook to Hazelden, a Minnesota-based nationwide continuum of programs and services to help the chemically addicted. I continue to admire the work that is accomplished there, and I continue to speak publicly about my disease, taking special enjoyment in sharing my story with young people. It was after just such a presentation when a young woman came up to me and asked, "If you could choose anything to write on your headstone, what would it be?" I'm not sure what she expected as an answer. Perhaps she thought I would brag about the success of A-dec. Instead, I answered, "I was able to become the person God intended for me to be." I have come to understand, however, that answer was incorrect. I know in my heart that each day is a spiritual journey. I have not become anything. I am only becoming the person God meant me to be.

*Here I am modeling my Class of '53 letterman's sweater
next to my favorite '39 Ford.*

CHAPTER 12

A BOY AND HIS CARS

Had I grown up in or near Detroit, I have absolutely no doubt that my entire working life would have been spent in the auto industry. The fact that a tiny amount of gasoline could release an incredible amount of energy in an internal combustion engine fascinated me from my earliest days on the farm, and that fascination—along with the hours I devoted to spending time under the hood of a car—only increased each year as I grew up. (Or, as Joan correctly pointed out, when it came to cars, I never grew up.)

I was just fourteen years old when I got my first car—the 1928 Chevy I bought after receiving my driver's permit. One year later, I traded it in for a 1928 Model A Ford Coupe; I traded that in the next year for a 1930 Ford Roadster; and two years later I replaced that Ford with another—a 1936 four-door sedan. I sold the sedan in 1949 for four hundred dollars when I went off to college, using three hundred dollars for tuition and room and board and the leftover hundred dollars to buy a 1928 Ford Model A pick up.

My preference for Fords was due to the fact that Henry Ford believed his cars should have interchangeable parts, so that you could upgrade older vehicles with parts from newer models. For instance, I was able to take a 1932 Ford V-8 engine and put it in my 1928 Ford model with only slight modification.

Some more treasures from my collection.

In other words, if tinkering with and modifying cars to allow them to go faster was your thing—and it was mine—then Ford was your car, and hot-rodding was your hobby.

I had the good fortune of having my automotive coming of age coincide with the beginning of the hot rod craze. The term *hot rods* gained popularity in the late 1930s and early 1940s when people would race their modified cars on dry lakebeds near Los Angeles. Before long, a magazine devoted to the modifying of cars was being published, and I read every issue from cover to cover.

It was an easy step from building and fixing hot rods to wanting to race them, and many summer days and weekends during my college years were spent behind the wheel at drag races. I especially recall a journey to the Bonneville Salt Flats in Utah, where, in the summer of 1952, I recorded a speed of 115.86 miles per hour in what is undoubtedly the automobile that has meant the most to me. It is a white 1939 Ford convertible sedan that I bought as a freshman at OSC after it

became clear that my Model A truck was good for hauling boxes and luggage back and forth to college, but it wasn't worth a darn in terms of attracting coeds. The sedan had been used to drive the Portland Rose Festival Queen in the 1939 Rose Festival Parade, and it was a beaut. Joan and I went on many dates in that car, and she spent countless hours with me in the Rod Shop as I installed a new engine before driving it to Utah. We took it at a much more leisurely pace the next year when Joan and I drove it to Vancouver, British Columbia, on our honeymoon. I sold the car after graduating from college and before entering the military but was reunited with it over two decades later in 1976, when Joan tracked it down, bought it, and gave it to me as a surprise Christmas present! It continues to draw admiring looks and whistles when it is occasionally used to transport a bride and groom from the church to their wedding reception.

The sedan now joins more than thirty antique and classic cars and trucks as part of a private museum located near A-dec headquarters. Also included in the collection is a replica of the

In my favorite car with my favorite lady. We drove this 1939 Ford to Canada on our honeymoon. Decades later, Joan tracked the car down and gave it to me as a surprise Christmas present.

Ford Model T hot rod built the summer after my freshman year at OSC to prove to myself that I was better than my classroom grades suggested. I built the car in the Rod Shop, using a 1927 Model T body and souping it up with a mixture of parts from other cars. This is the car I was racing in Eugene when my then-girlfriend gave me the ultimatum of choosing between racing and her, and the car with no floorboards, in which I picked up Joan for our first official date. With Joan as my pit boss, I would hit 106.7 miles per hour at a drag strip near Aurora, Oregon.

Maintaining an antique and classic automobile collection is a job that is much too big for me, and I am indebted to Mike

Peterson, Al Lyda, and Paul Sturges—three incredibly talented gentlemen who share my love of all things automotive and who never met a car they couldn't repair or restore.

One of the benefits of giving up day-to-day control of A-dec is that it has given me more time to be a gearhead. Several years ago, I was asked by Ron Love, a longtime friend, to build a manifold, which is the part of the engine that conveys air and fuel from the carburetor to the cylinders. Paul Sturges also assisted me in building the manifold. We had such a good time that we ran an advertisement to see if anyone else needed a custom-built manifold, and we received quite a few responses. By the time I sold my little manifold business to H & H Flatheads in 2014, we were offering twenty-one different intake manifolds for Ford engines.

In April of 2014, I took time away from catching up on manifold orders to fly to Burbank, California, for a close-up look at the garage of my dreams—the garage where former *Tonight Show* host Jay Leno stores his remarkable automobile collection. Jay was incredibly kind with his time, and if there wasn't a plane to catch to return to Oregon, I would probably still be in his garage, tinkering with his "toys."

Joan dreamed of building a world-class inn and spa in Newberg. Her vision and leadership turned that dream into a reality: The Allison.

CHAPTER 13

A GIRL AND HER HOTEL

Because Joan was so humble and unassuming, people often tended to underestimate her abilities. This was especially true in the early years of A-dec, as women executives were nonexistent in the dental equipment industry. As we attended our first industry conventions and trade shows, the dismissive looks she received from other attendees were easy to spot. She took it all in stride, however, and as A-dec grew and prospered, and as she filled public roles like being the first woman to serve as chairman of Associated Oregon Industries—the state's oldest and largest business lobby— and the first woman appointed to the Oregon Economic Development Commission, her abilities became more appreciated and admired. And with the opening of The Allison Inn & Spa in September 2009, Joan's vision, intelligence, perseverance, and leadership skills became obvious to all.

In just five years of operation, the eighty-five-room Allison has rapidly earned a reputation as one of most outstanding hotels in the world. You don't have to take my word for that. You can take the word of respected travel services like AAA, Fodor's, and Trip Advisor, and publications like *Forbes*, *Conde Nast Traveler*, and *Travel and Leisure*—all of which have showered The Allison with awards and top-of-the-industry rankings.

The path that led to The Allison was one that began in the mid 1980s, when Joan and I were working with Dr. Neff to build the Springbrook facility. At the time, family members and friends of those receiving treatment at Springbrook had few lodging options if they wanted to stay in Newberg to offer help and support to loved ones. Joan and I had acquired and pieced together a number of parcels of land on a beautiful hill overlooking Springbrook, and she began to dream of building a little twenty-five-bed country inn. At her urging, we took a few steps to make that dream a reality, including obtaining the appropriate governmental approvals and building permits. Everything was put on the back burner, however, when Shilo Inns, a popular lodging company in the Pacific Northwest, built and opened a motel in midtown Newberg. Joan and I concluded that two new motels was one too many.

Joan once reflected, "Dreams have a way of growing. Even when you put them away for a while, they can grow." Twenty years after shelving her original plan to build a small country inn, two changes occurred that led Joan to begin dreaming of something bigger. The first change was that we had continued to acquire land in the area, eventually piecing together 550 acres. The second change was that Newberg and the Yamhill Valley had become ground zero for the remarkable boom in the Oregon wine industry. When A-dec opened in 1964, there were no commercial wineries or vineyards in Yamhill County. Today, the county boasts well over three hundred wineries and vineyards, and wine tourism has become one of the region's leading industries. Joan and I would often hear frustrated local business leaders observe that wine connoisseurs would come into the area for the day and return to Portland hotels in the evening. What was needed, they said, was a destination inn that would keep these visitors—and their money—in Newberg and Yamhill County.

The more we heard, the more Joan began to dream, and the more excited she became—in spite of the fact that her husband was not very supportive. We know everything there is to know about the dental equipment business, I told Joan, but we don't know a thing about what it takes to succeed in the hospitality business. Before I knew it, Joan had put together a team of advisors who each had a track record of success in the lodging industry. Their advice and counsel were tremendously helpful to Joan, and I could see from the gleam in her eyes and the smile on her face that she had found a calling.

The Allison was to be front and center in Joan's life from the groundbreaking in October 2007 to its opening in September 2009. I have never been more proud of her as I watched her expertly navigate through the seemingly endless array of big and small decisions that needed to be made in the design and construction process. While many individuals had a voice in these decisions, she always had the deciding vote, and the end result is pure 100 percent Joan. To ensure that she could see and feel the quality of everything that would be going into each of the eighty-five Allison guest rooms, Joan had a model room created. The room was the actual size of the standard king room and contained all of the exact furnishings.

Joan wanted The Allison not just to be *in* Yamhill County but to be *of* Yamhill County. Local contractors were used to the greatest degree possible, providing employment and family-wage jobs to the region. Local farms and local wineries provide the produce and wine used by Jory, the award-winning six-thousand-square-foot restaurant in The Allison. And over one hundred local artists produced the more than five hundred pieces of art that are displayed throughout the inn, curated by our daughter, Loni. When construction was completed, Joan and Loni inspected every guest room, and the two of them oversaw the installment of artwork in each room. Our son, Ken III, who is an expert woodworker, also left his mark on The Allison, personally handcrafting tables for the inn's rooms and restaurant.

Oregon is a state with a tremendous environmental ethic, and Joan also made sure The Allison reflected that ethic. It is one of only twenty-five hotels in the world to achieve gold-level Leadership in Energy and Environmental Design (LEED) certification.

Joan was immensely proud of the success of The Allison, and immensely proud of the more than two hundred Allison employees who have become like family to us. The times we spent there in the last four years of her life were some of the most enjoyable and satisfying of our sixty years together. Those who knew and loved Joan tell me frequently that they can feel her presence when they visit The Allison. I can, too.

CHAPTER 14

ADVENTURES IN THE WHITE HOUSE

I'm sure if you were to ask someone to name a career that is most likely to provide the opportunity to visit the White House and the Presidential retreat at Camp David, manufacturing dental equipment would not be the response that would come to mind. The fact is, however, that at some time or another, everyone is in need of dental care—even the president of the United States.

During President Clinton's administration, Joan and I were in Washington, DC, for a business association gathering and were part of a special tour of the White House. During the tour, I happened to mention to a White House usher that my company had recently provided the equipment for the dentist's office located in the White House. I saw him whisper this information to another usher, who I'm sure whispered it to a Secret Service agent, who probably quickly did a computer check on my background, as a few minutes later, the usher retrieved Joan and me and personally escorted us on a brief visit to see our equipment.

A few years later, Joan and I attended an event in Portland for Texas Governor George W. Bush, who was then seeking the 2000 Presidential nomination of the Republican Party. A-dec had recently delivered a large order of equipment to the

A day we will always remember—touring the presidential retreat at Camp David, which includes a dental office full of A-dec equipment.

dental school at the University of Texas, so as Joan and I were introduced to President Bush in the photo line, I thanked him for his business, and told him that if he were elected, we would be proud to update the dental equipment in the White House.

In January 2001, Joan and I were privileged to attend President Bush's inauguration in Washington. The first morning after we returned to Newberg, I spoke to a group of United States military technicians who were attending an A-dec training class and began my remarks by apologizing for missing the opening reception for the class the previous evening. After explaining that I had missed the reception because I was in Washington, DC, one of the technicians said that he had been there, as well. As we talked further, I mentioned my earlier visit to the White House, and he asked if A-dec could provide equipment to the dental office at Camp David. I must not have been listening closely, as when I heard the word *Camp*, I thought he meant a large military base like Camp Pendleton that was home to thousands of marines. "That must be a very large order," I said. "No," he explained. "It only has *two* chairs." It finally dawned on me that the camp he was mentioning was indeed Camp David, the exclusive presidential retreat. A few months later, Joan and I kept pinching ourselves that two farm kids from Newberg somehow found themselves at Camp David, cutting the ribbon that officially opened a new, modernized presidential dental office.

Joan and I helped cut the ribbon at the Camp David dental office.

Scott Parrish is absolutely the right person to lead A-dec to new heights.

CHAPTER 15

FAMILY BUSINESS DYNAMICS

Whenever a young person asked Joan to share some advice on the secret to a successful life, she would often reply, "Life is too short to do something you don't enjoy. Go find what you love and then give it everything you've got." Since the afternoon we drove back home from that Colorado picnic knowing we were starting a business even if we had to live on bread and beans, Joan and I were fortunate to live her words. We loved watching our company grow; we loved working with our employees, our vendors, and our customers; and we loved giving it everything we had.

Joan and I were in our early thirties when we started A-dec, and we continued to pour our heart and soul into the company as we went through our forties, our fifties, our sixties, and into our seventies. As the years sped by, however, we also found enjoyment in activities that took us away from the day-to-day operations of the business. Joan was increasingly busy with the endless tasks necessary to getting The Allison up and running. I enjoyed spending time in my workshop and tinkering with some of my cars, and both of us were dedicated to our philanthropic work.

In 2007, it became clear to both of us that it was time to hand the management of A-dec over to a younger generation. Fortunately, we had a perfect candidate in Scott Parrish, our son-in-law. Joan and I understood, however, that A-dec was a business, not a dynasty, and we didn't want our familial connection to Scott to get in the way of the right decision for the future success of the company. Therefore, we asked a team of outside advisors to study the situation and to recommend a candidate who could assume the role of president and chief operating officer. The team unanimously recommended Scott, who began working at A-dec in 1986, as the most qualified.

I wish it could be said that I did everything in my power to make the transition to Scott an easy one, but that would be miles away from the truth. The fact is that I spent a good part of the next three years, trying to make Scott's life much more difficult than it needed to be.

The problem was my ego—the same ego that led to the numerous false starts and firings early my career. As I watched Scott make decisions, I became upset that he wasn't making the same decisions I would have made. Joan was much more successful at giving Scott room to run the business as he saw fit, urging me to leave him alone and to accept the fact that we were no longer in charge. I suppose that down deep I knew she was right, but I continued to envision myself as A-dec's benevolent dictator, where I still pulled the puppet strings.

Needless to say, having me constantly second-guess his decisions and occasionally going behind his back to countermand those decisions were not Scott's idea of a good time. The fact that Scott was married to our daughter also made the situation even more awkward. To her credit, however, Loni steered clear of our conflict, knowing that we needed to work through it ourselves.

Believe it or not, what finally led me to see the error of my ways was a flat tire. Joan and I were attending a company sales dinner at a hotel near Newberg when an A-dec sales representative came up to me and asked how I was doing. I proceeded to tell him that I wasn't doing very well, and how upset I was at some of Scott's decisions. I knew it was absolutely the wrong thing to do, but I continued to vent. A short time later, a few A-dec employees made a beeline to me and explained that they had just come from the hotel parking lot and noticed that Joan's car had a flat tire. They volunteered to change the tire and asked for the car keys so they could access the trunk to retrieve the spare. Near the end of the evening, Joan asked me to go out to the car to retrieve an item she had left in the trunk. When I opened the trunk and saw the flat tire that had been placed there so carefully, I burst out in tears, as it dawned on me that the people at A-dec still cared for us, and that nobody—including Scott—was trying to undermine us. When the sales meeting reconvened the next morning, I took to the podium and explained through tears that a flat tire had changed my life. I promised Scott and his team that they had my complete loyalty and support. It is a promise I have always kept.

CHAPTER 16

THE NEXT FIFTY YEARS

February 2015 marks fifty years since A-dec opened for business in that Newberg Quonset hut. Writing this book has allowed me the opportunity to share the story of A-dec's past. What is far more important to me, however—and what was far more important to Joan— is A-dec's future.

While I know I won't be around when A-dec celebrates its 100th anniversary in the year 2065, it is my profound hope that the following four statements will come to pass.

First, A-dec will remain headquartered in Newberg. Over the course of time, Joan and I watched as many Oregon companies were acquired and moved out of the state. We were immensely proud of the role that A-dec played in the economic growth of Yamhill County and the family-wage jobs it has provided to thousands of individuals. There was never a moment when we envisioned that our company would leave the community that had been so good to us and that we loved so much.

Second, a new A-dec employee hired in 2065 will still be expected to learn the A-dec Way, and those fifteen principles will remain as the company's guiding philosophy.

Third, the A-dec of 2065 will be regarded as it is today—as a business that is on the cutting edge of the dental equipment industry. Just as dentistry has changed in countless ways over the past half century, it will change in even more ways in the years to come. While I can't imagine the technological innovations that await, I can imagine that they will be ones that were created at A-dec.

Finally, I am confident that those first three statements will be true if this one is true: In 2065, A-dec will still be in Austin family ownership. By that, I don't mean that my five grandchildren—Matt, Grant, Ashley, Todd, or Jessica—or their children or their children's children must work full-time at A-dec. They should each have the right to pursue their own individual dreams, to find a career they love, and to give it everything they have, just as Joan and I did. What I do mean, however, is that family members will honor their heritage by remaining active and interested owners and will ensure that the day-to-day managers of A-dec are guiding the company in the right direction and with the right values.

In short, for fifty years, A-dec has taken care of our employees, our customers, and our community. May it always be so.

CHAPTER 17

IN JOAN'S WORDS

When A-dec celebrated its thirty-fifth anniversary, Joan and I were asked a series of questions by the editors of *On-Dec*, our company magazine that is published quarterly to encourage open and regular communication with our employees, retirees, and friends. Our answers to those questions were printed in a special anniversary edition of the magazine. I recently found a copy of that edition, and as I read Joan's answers, I could clearly hear her voice. This book wouldn't be complete if you didn't hear it, too.

What is your essential business philosophy? *Believing in what you are doing, and with that comes honesty, integrity, fairness, determination, and dedication. Very important through all of that is caring.*

What is your guiding principle? *Doing the very best I know how to do with what is available; finishing what I start, and in so doing, trying to learn something new each day.*

What is the best way to keep a competitive edge? *We at A-dec have been a leader for so many years that it's hard to think of anything other than being the first with innovative and creative ideas that make dependable and quality products for our customers. Quality and customer service are of utmost importance. Knowing your competition is also important.*

*The love of my life. I was privileged to be her husband
for one week short of sixty years.*

What is your yardstick for success? *A yardstick for success is feeling good about myself and my accomplishments, whatever they may be. I have always said success is to be able to look in a mirror and say, "I'm okay and I like me."*

What is a goal yet to be achieved? *There are two major items. The first is to prepare A-dec and its employees for transition to the day when Ken and I retire to pursue other interests. Secondly, I am a land lover. Through the years we have accumulated considerable acreage around A-dec. It is important for me to see that it is developed in the way that is both effective and beneficial to both its neighbors and to the community.* [Not surprisingly, Joan successfully achieved these goals.]

What has been your best business decision? *To me, that's a slam-dunk: The decision to begin A-dec; encouraging Ken to step out and start the company; telling him I would be his partner and that we would build the company together.*

What has been your worst business decision? *I am not going to give you a worst decision because I don't know what it would be. We have always tried to talk things through to see the effect that the decision would have and so maybe in many instances the terrible consequences have been averted. I do feel badly, however, when I override my intuition and find things go awry. I always look at that and think, "Why didn't I follow that intuition?"*

What was the toughest business decision? *Cutting off our largest customer, who at the time was 18 percent of our business. It was a tough decision to make, but it was the right one to make, and our other customers jumped in and made up that 18 percent immediately.*

Did you have a mentor? *Yes. I started first grade when I was four, so I was very young when I graduated from high school. There was no money for college, so I went to work at an insurance company.*

My boss, the manager of the company, took me "under his wing," so to speak, and during a five-year period put me through every department of the insurance company and kept encouraging me to look forward to becoming an insurance agent and having my own agency. I had left that company under his watchful eye and went to work for an office in Newberg and managed that office. It was at that point I would have started off on my own, but then Ken came along and so that was really the end of my insurance career. So that mentor played a very big part in my life along with the encouragement he gave me to continue and to learn and to go forward.

What has been the most important lesson you have learned? *To hang in there, to finish what you start. It feels so good to complete something, knowing that you have done your best.*

What is your favorite quote? *Do unto others what you would have them do unto you.*

What is the most influential book you have read? *The Bible.*

What is your favorite way to spend free time? *I need rebuilding time—a time to be alone, to take a good close look at my inner self and to see who I am, where I am, and if this is where I want to be. Family time is also very, very important to me. We have a very close, happy family, and it's fun to be with them.*

What do you see as the future for A-dec? *We have been a leader for so many years, it's hard to think of anything other than being the first with innovative and creative ideas that make dependable and quality products for our customers.*

Is there anything else you would like to share? *I have been blessed in so many ways. Ken and I have had a wonderful life. We have a beautiful family that we are so very proud of, and have loved watching our grandchildren grow to become their own* *individuals. It has been very gratifying to build a successful company together. It has been most rewarding to watch our employees grow in their knowledge and abilities and to better themselves. I take a great deal of pride in watching those employees grow. It is a great feeling to be able to contribute to our community and state, not necessarily with money, but with time and effort. The giving back is so very important to me.*

THE WIFE OF NOBLE CHARACTER

The love people held for Joan was movingly displayed on the beautiful summer morning of June 15, 2013, when an audience of over one thousand gathered in a field down the hill from The Allison for her memorial service. The service included Joan's favorite music, performed by the Oregon Symphony Orchestra, her friends and A-dec employees Farrah Burke and Marion Pettis, and a wonderful group of students who attended the Joan Austin Elementary School. It also included touching remarks from each of our five grandchildren, and an eloquent eulogy from our great friend, George Fox University President Robin Baker. Knowing that my emotions would get the best of me, I chose not to speak at the service and asked President Baker to read a letter that I had written. I also requested Pastor Tom Struck to read a Bible verse, which encompassed all that Joan meant to me. My letter and the Bible verse follow:

A HUSBAND'S TRIBUTE

Thank you all for being here today to honor Joan. I would like to share with you some of my memories of Joan.

She was truly a farmer's daughter, and that never changed. She told me she helped her dad with the chores of a family farm. With a saddened heart, she spoke of the tough times on the farm in Minnesota and how her dad came in the house with tears in his eyes and said that the crops were ruined from that day's hail storm. They would need to sell everything and move to Oregon, where some of their friends and neighbors had moved to in 1941 to work in the shipyards. They lived in Vanport for a short time before settling in Dundee.

That move didn't change her much. Joan, along with her brothers and sisters, would work in the fields around Newberg picking berries to earn money for school clothes. I can't imagine how she looked back then.

After graduating from Newberg High School in 1948, she began searching for a job and a career that she would enjoy.

After working in Portland a year or so, she found that career in a small Newberg insurance office. Her first dream was beginning to come true until June 2, 1952, when I managed to get an arranged date with Joan through her sister's boyfriend.

None of you can imagine how she looked on that first date. No makeup. Hair up in big rollers. Hawaiian shirt, an old pair of jeans, and flip flops!

She said later that if I wanted to date her, I needed to call her and not her sister's boyfriend.

That was lesson number one. There have been many lessons learned since that first date six decades ago.

The last thing I remember was on the night of June 4, 2013, when she told me she loved me so much and to have sweet dreams. Then she asked, "Are you sure the cat is in the house? You let him out and he hasn't come in the bedroom yet."

I went to check and found the cat eating his evening snack. She was in control to the last minute.

I am not sure who she worried the most about—the cat or me. I know she loved all things and in particular she loved animals. I knew I was going to be cared for back in 1952 when she told me on our first date that I was just like a little, lost puppy.

We have held hands for sixty-one years and three days, and I will always hold her in my heart until The Lord lets me hold her hand again in Heaven.

I would like to share with you some of her dreams.

- To have a good and long-lasting marriage. We were eight days short of sixty years.
- She loved babies.
- She had a desire to help others and not herself regardless of who they were. Even some democrats!
- To help others get a formal education because she couldn't afford to go to college.
- To take care of sick and stray animals.
- To have a strong relationship with God and country.
- To preserve the precious gemstones, history, nature, and beauty.
- To be a land lover, and she acquired over fifty acres all around where you are seated now.
- She dreamed of having her own business. We did.
- She worked hard on making the right decisions.
- She believed in family-owned businesses.
- She wanted The Allison to be a treasure to Yamhill County and to Oregon, and her dream has come true.

Thank you, God, for sharing Joan with all of us. Thank you, God, for everything.

Love, Ken
June 15, 2013

PROVERBS 31: 10-31

A wife of noble character who can find? She is worth far more than rubies. Her husband has full confidence in her and lacks nothing of value. She brings him good, not harm, all the days of her life. She selects wool and flax and works with eager hands. She is like the merchant ships, bringing her food from afar. She gets up while it is still night; she provides food for her family and portions for her female servants. She considers a field and buys it; out of her earnings she plants a vineyard. She sets about her work vigorously; her arms are strong for her tasks. She sees that her trading is profitable, and her lamp does not go out at night. In her hand she holds the distaff and grasps the spindle with her fingers. She opens her arms to the poor and extends her hands to the needy. When it snows, she has no fear for her household; for all of them are clothed in scarlet. She makes coverings for her bed; she is clothed in fine linen and purple. Her husband is respected at the city gate, where he takes his seat among the elders of the land. She makes linen garments and sells them, and supplies the merchants with sashes. She is clothed with strength and dignity; she can laugh at the days to come. She speaks with wisdom, and faithful instruction is on her tongue. She watches over the affairs of her household and does not eat the bread of idleness. Her children arise and call her blessed; her husband also, and he praises her, "Many women do noble things, but you surpass them all." Charm is deceptive, and beauty is fleeting; but a woman who fears the Lord is to be praised. Honor her for all that her hands have done, and let her works bring her praise at the city gate.

An Editorial Tribute

Oregon's leading newspaper, the *Oregonian*, saluted Joan's life and legacy in the following June 10, 2013, editorial:

It's easy to forget during the heat of a legislative session that it takes more than good policies to make a state succeed. It also takes extraordinary people like Joan Austin, who died last week just days short of the 60th anniversary of her marriage to Ken Austin. The couple built one of the world's largest manufacturers of dental equipment and, just as importantly, a legacy of philanthropy and community involvement that reaches across the state from their hometown of Newberg.

The family business, A-dec Inc., is the product of hard work and some good fortune, explains Ken, as "I had problems working for other companies." After losing a job in Colorado, he proposed that the young family move back to Oregon to manufacture a vacuum-powered dental device. "She said within moments, 'I'll help you even if we have to live on bread and beans,'" he recalls.

Joan, who had worked in the insurance industry, handled the business side of the enterprise while Ken developed products. They aspired initially to have 10 employees within five years, but met that mark within nine months. After a decade, says Ken, the company employed 140 people. Now, about 50 years after its founding, A-dec has almost 1,000 employees in Newberg and 1,100 worldwide.

With success came the ability to give, and give the Austins have in abundance. Beneficiaries of the family's largess include libraries, arts organizations and, perhaps most significantly, schools. When Oregon State University started a family business program back in the 1980s, finding the money to support it was a struggle, says university President Ed Ray. Then, the Austins stepped into help—and kept right on helping. Two of the University's signature business programs now carry the family name: the Austin Entrepreneurship Program and the Austin Family Business Program.

Nowhere, however, is Joan Austin's personal style of philanthropy more in evidence than at Joan Austin Elementary in Newberg. In 2002, the Austins gave voters an incentive to support a $46 million bond that would, among other things, pay for a new elementary school. If the bond passed, the family promised to donate a 10-acre parcel of land for the new school. The bond did pass, of course, and the school board subsequently named the school after Joan Austin...but the story doesn't end there.

Joan Austin got involved at the school—and stayed involved. She worked with architects and the district during construction, helping, for instance, choose the flooring and colors, says Lesley Carsley, the school's first principal. After the school opened, she welcomed each incoming kindergarten class with a tea party in the school library. The tradition, complete with cookies, china and sugar cubes, "was a wonderful way for students to start their experience at Joan Austin Elementary," recalls Carsley.

Joan Austin also chose the motto inscribed in the entryway floor: "Education grants us the knowledge to pursue our dreams," which must have carried particular significance for her. Ken Austin is an Oregon State alumnus, and Joan became deeply involved with the school in adulthood, serving for many years on the OSU Foundation Board of Trustees. But Joan didn't have the money to go to college herself.

Instead, she went to work and built a life that exemplifies what daughter Loni Austin Parrish says she expected of her children: "do our best, work hard, and give back to others."

ACKNOWLEDGMENTS

I have long been blessed with individuals who provided assistance and guidance at key moments in my life and career. Thankfully, this was also the case in completing this book.

I begin by thanking George Edmonston Jr., who previously spent countless hours in researching and cataloging Joan's and my history and the history of A-dec. This book would not have been possible without his efforts.

Kerry Tymchuk took George's material and worked with me over many months to turn it into a book that is truly mine. Some had warned me that producing a book would be a chore, but Kerry made the process very enjoyable and rewarding.

My gratitude also goes out to Lisa Thompson, who kept the book moving forward by organizing my schedule, and who also provided great assistance in digging through old files and photographs.

I shared the manuscript of the book with many close friends, and each made suggestions that ultimately improved the final product.

Dr. Ed Ray honored me by agreeing to write the foreword. Oregon State University is for the better because of his stellar leadership, and I am for the better because he is my friend.

There is no other company I would rather have publish this book than Oregon State University Press, and I appreciate the expertise that Tom Booth offered in the publishing process.